HOW TO FLY

For People Who Are
Not Sure They Want To

GORDON BAXTER

DRAWINGS BY THE AUTHOR

SUMMIT BOOKS
NEW YORK

Published by *Summit Books*
A Simon & Schuster Division of Gulf & Western Corporation
Simon & Schuster Building
Rockefeller Center
1230 Avenue of the Americas
New York, New York 10020
SUMMIT BOOKS and colophon are trademarks of Simon & Schuster
Designed by Stanley S. Drate
Manufactured in the United States of America
1 3 5 7 9 10 8 6 4 2

Library of Congress Cataloging in Publication Data

Baxter, Gordon
How to fly.

Includes index.
1. Airplanes—Piloting. 2. Private flying. I. Title.
TL710.B39   629.132′5217   81–9369
                                      AACR2

ISBN 0–671–44801–3

To Ray C. Gannaway
and
to Alfred G. Vanneman,
instructors,
who risked those first ten hours
of flight with me.

ACKNOWLEDGMENTS

With thanks to Bob and Kathy Walker. They took over as FBO at Beaumont Municipal Airport after Lee "Pappy" Sheffield retired and the famous old grass airport was lighted, paved, and got its radio beacon. The Walkers retained the gentle hospitality that ole Pappy is best remembered for.

Bob Walker, professional pilot, used his knowledge as a Certified Flight Instructor, Instrument and Multi-Engine, to edit the technical aspects of this work.

Kathy Walker typed the manuscript while running the office and radios, there within the sights and sounds of airplanes at the homeplate of this story.

CONTENTS

FOREWORD

Melissa Thigpen said, "I can learn more in the airplane than I can reading about it . . . especially if I can't understand what I'm reading."

The old flight instructor said, "The romance of flying brings them out here; the book we give them chills them."

Betty Em Giarrantano said, "They sent me home with a book that looked like engineering notes. I never went back. That was the kind of stuff I was hoping to fly away from."

This book is not so much intended to teach you all about how to fly as it is to increase your *desire* to fly and to give you some idea of what to expect out at the airport.

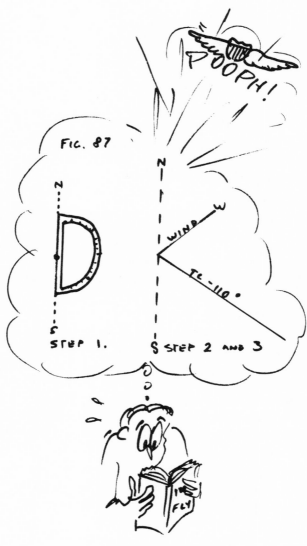

"I never went back."

1

NEW BOY
AT THIS CLUB

Wilbur Wright may have said it better than any of us when he came down from that first flight in that first airplane. The taciturn and properly business-suited Wilbur said of his invention: "More than anything else, the sensation is one of perfect peace, mingled with an excitement that strains every nerve to the utmost, if you can conceive of such a combination."

To me flying is mostly an experience in beauty. In my twenty-five years as a pilot, flying has scared me, flying has bored me, flying has emptied my pockets. I read and dreamed flying most of my life but I never got up the nerve to go out to the airport and ask someone to teach me how to fly until I was thirty-three years old, and then had to overcome the humiliation of getting airsick.

The things I have learned have held true through all my years of flying little airplanes. Nothing having to do with aviation seems to diminish a person's character. And no matter what nagging devils seem to be chasing their tails through your mind as you go out to the airport, the world somehow seems saner after you have escaped from it awhile and then descended to it again on your own terms.

To fly a light plane, especially alone, is to be in touch with some honesty, some near-mystic force, that eludes description in words. Even the junkyards look orderly from above.

The person you are looking for at the airport is the FBO, which stands for *fixed base operator.** The fixed base operator was so called to differentiate him from the fly-by-nighter, or *barnstormer*, whose days ended as recently as the 1930s. It was slow going, earning a living with an airplane then, and the barnstormer was just trading on the novelty of it. Flying south in the winter, taking people up for thrill rides, operating out of his hip pocket and rear cockpit.

My own first rides were with barnstormers in the sunset of what is now called the golden age of aviation. The distant sound of an airplane engine in the then-empty sky brought us pummeling our bike pedals to the pasture. "Airplane! Airplane!" we would shout, curving our bicycles down the dust of the country road, our eyes to the sky. The *biplane* would circle lower, growing larger in our dreams. The pilot would make a low pass or two along the length of the pasture, his leather-helmeted head out in the *slipstream*, peering down through his goggles looking for grass-hidden ditches or other obstacles that might damage his plane upon landing, and getting a good estimate of the *surface winds* and the distance available to stop in. This is still the prudent

---

* Flying has its own terms of art. Its special vocabulary, though not as formidable as the arcane jargon of the legal and medical professions, is sufficiently obscure to require a glossary. Throughout this text, I italicize terms whenever I think they may not be clear to some readers. All such italicized terms are defined in the glossary, which also includes a few terms you might see or hear elsewhere.

behavior of any pilot about to settle onto unknown turf.

We would stand captured by the art of his landing. You see this at the airports today; few pilots can resist pausing to watch another pilot land. Solemnly the biplane would turn onto its *final approach*, descending, the song of its engine reduced to a muttering. The sun would catch a flash of its *propeller* blades, and glint from its *wings*. Without the aid of *flaps* to reduce *airspeed*, the pilot in those days fluttered earthward in a ballet of delicate little control movements—sometimes *fishtailing*, always in a graceful *slip*, a maneuver you will come to love and which is still useful today. With this pilot it was a matter of slipping the airplane a little sideways to see down the side beyond his engine. In your turn you will be seated up front, behind the windshield with a fine panoramic view ahead. The old birds landed blind as a bat. When he eased back the *joystick* and sighed gracefully into the grass, his *cowling* rose upward and the engine blocked out all forward view. He would *taxi* smartly to a stop, rise up in the *cockpit*, lifting his goggles to his forehead, with their red imprints still in his cheeks, and grin at us. He was our god descended right out of the heavens.

We raced on our bikes, because he picked the first boys that got there to guard the plane that night in exchange for the first ride next day. I never smell oil of citronella without a memory of those humid, mosquito-filled nights in the cockpit of some barnstormer's plane, clutching the stick, flying oceans with Lindbergh, feeling the taut, easy tensions in the controls as I moved them in the dark, and dreaming of how good it would be to someday do this for real. And you know, it *was* that good. Still is.

The advertising and business methods of the barnstormer were quite simple. At dawn next day he rose up and went flying low down main street, beat up the town, let them know that an airplane was here. They came out, brought their Kodaks, bought a few five-dollar rides. The pilot would stay as long as he could make it pay. Sometimes a young blade of the town would ask for flying lessons. That was actually steady income for the barnstormer. Sometimes a visionary businessman would see how the airplane could get him into the city, so he could do his business and get back while his competitors were still waiting for the train. And he would daringly charter a flight. This business-and-aviation getting-acquainted process is still going on.

If the barnstormer hit a good town, as Glenn Parker did in my town of Port Arthur, Texas, he stayed. He leased or bought the pasture. It became Parker's Airport. He built an operations shack. He had become a fixed base operator.

The leather-jacketed gypsy pilot, the barnstormer, brought personal flying to America. The airlines and the new DC-3 brought transportation. The distinction between the two at the airports still remains. Don't go to the airline terminal to ask to learn how to fly, go find the FBO.

The hip-pocket business characteristics of the barnstormer can still be found in the face the FBO presents to the public today. If the average retailer were to conduct his business along the lines of the average airplane store he would soon go under, as many of the FBOs historically do.

The FBO does not think of himself as an "airplane store." He usually does not advertise, promote, or even leap up and greet you at the door with a "May I help you?" He thinks of himself first as an aviator. A pilot, who is just doing all this charter flying, airplane renting, and student instruction to keep him and his true love, the airplane, together at night.

He still sees himself somewhat as we first saw him

when he stood up in the cockpit of that biplane and raised his goggles and grinned down at us. The message was, "If you boys are really worthy, I will let you enter into all this with me."

Although the cost is much the same, walking into the airplane store to buy flying lessons is not going to be very much like walking into the car store to buy a new Cadillac. Aside from indifference, there is outright snobbery of the kind that smites any "new boy" at the golf pro shop or at the sailing marina. As in any other form of clubhouse snobbery the atmosphere is greatly improved if an old member of this club brings you out as a personal friend and handshakes you all around.

A thaw will begin as soon as they see that you are serious about wanting to learn how to fly. You will become a full member of this club as soon as you come in, shaking your head and laughing, from your first hour of instruction. They will be laughing with you, not at you, and you will soon sense that there is a comradely protection extended toward the student from the entire aviation community. Everything that you do as a beginner happened to us, too, and the memory stays scented green forever.

So don't feel cut dead when you first walk into the FBO shack out at the airport and nobody looks up. Just go on and say those awful words loudly and clearly to the assembly gathered there: "Who do I see around here to take flying lessons?"

You probably had to ask around the airport to find the FBO; now you will have to ask the FBO if he will take you up flying for a demonstration ride. Nearly all of them want to sit down over papers with you first, explain the costs, then send you home with the book, the kit, the brochure, whatever, and you will still not have tasted the sweet fruit of what this is all about. Will flying scare you? Delight you? Be an overrated experience? Like the virgin turning from reading romance to the actual experience, could flying possibly be as good as all this heavy-breathing aviation romance that we write about it?

Unlike any other form of retail business that I can think of, coming into the FBO, the "airplane store," puts a lot of the burden of aggressiveness onto the customer.

Perhaps aviation's coy attitude of "If you can catch me you can kiss me" is our subconscious way of still saying that there really is something special about flying that sets us apart and this is our first test of many to see if you are really worthy.

This thing of setting out to earn your wings is going to make heavy demands on your time and money. Not that the pursuit of this golden grail isn't worth it. Ask any pilot. Or see the little ceremony they hold when some silvered old captain of the line hits the now mandatory retirement age of sixty and flies his last scheduled run and steps down off the *flight deck* with tears in his eyes. How many careers can you think of where after a lifetime of work, the person dreads being separated from it?

I really do not know why you still have to invite yourself into aviation business. Whatever the reasons are, it's likely that nobody has bombarded you with much advertising and you have come this far on your own.

After you find the FBO, get someone to talk to you there, and persuade them to take you on a demonstration flight right now, you still have one more thing to ask for. Once you're away from the busy airport and the airplane settles down to cruise, the flight instructor usually invites you to fly it. If he doesn't, then ask for that, too.

Now let's try to describe what that first flight experience will be like.

WHO ME,
FLY THIS THING?

In all the good romance stories about flying, the pilot awakens first, now ignoring her smooth shoulders, and goes and stands in the doorway gazing at the sky. He sniffs the air for rain, notes and remembers the direction and force of the wind, casts a wary eye upon the height and movement of the clouds. Weather—that never tiring adversary he must soon come to solitary grips with.

This scene is not so easy to carry off with style if you live in an apartment and the door opens out to the elevators. But watch your flight instructor as you and he step out of the operations building and onto the *flight line*. If he does not cast a habitual and judgmental eye upon the sky, then either he has not been flying very long or he's been reading the wrong books.

If the *ceiling* is too low, or the winds too strong, he will tell you to come back another day.

Let your cheerful acceptance of nonflying weather be the first rule that will guide you evermore. Flying is not intrinsically dangerous, but too many good-running airplanes are driven into the ground by pilots who choose to continue on into adverse weather.

A definition of "adverse weather" must be qualified by the experience of the pilot and the equipment in his aircraft. At one end of the scale is the low-time student or *private pilot*, flying a small airplane which is equipped with only the most basic *flight instruments*. At the other extreme is the experienced three-man crew of a jet airliner which is fitted out with the most advanced *blind-flying* instruments, on-board radar, and *de-icing* devices.

Adverse weather has a widely different meaning to these two widely different segments of aviation, and to every level of experience and equipment in between. The basic line of demarcation, the one you will hear spoken the most, is *VFR* weather and *IFR* weather. VFR means *Visual Flight Rules*, a descriptive term that means the pilot will be able to see out the window and fly by visual reference to the ground. IFR means *Instrument Flight Rules*, which appropriately describes a plane and crew that can fly in clouds with no visual reference to the ground but instead can maintain controlled flight and navigate precisely by reference to instruments only.

VFR means there must be 3 miles visibility at the airport and the overcast, or cloud base level, must be at least 1,000 feet above ground. Away from the controlled airspace of an airport, VFR is a more relaxed 1-mile visibility and "clear of clouds."

The study of weather and the lifelong accumulation of weather flying judgment will be one of the most interesting and important parts of your entry into aviation.

So weather permitting, you and your pilot will walk out onto the flight line toward the *training plane*. Since the early 1930s, when the first good ones were developed, training planes are characteristically small, simple and sturdy of design, and easy and fun to fly. Without any stigma, like the training wheels on a bike, or training pants on a kid, training planes are often owned and flown just for the joy of it by pilots who earn a living flying airliners.

Your instructor will tell you what kind of a trainer this one is, and he will start the demonstration flight by describing what he is doing in the little *pre-flight* ceremony that we call the *walk-around* inspection.

Even the lofty airline captains send the *co-pilot* out in the cold to do this menial and repetitive chore. If, in your coming flying years, you ever see a pilot do what we contemptuously call "kick the tires and light the fires," you can discount him as a careless, foolish person.

This routine pre-flight inspection is important because there is just no easy way you can pull off the side of the road and look under the hood once you have gotten launched in an airplane.

The pilot will do the walk-around in a manner detailed for him in the owner's manual. Unlike the "owner's manual" which comes with a new car (really just a sales brochure), the aircraft owner's manual is full of engineering facts, data, operations charts, and performance tables. Its contents are the findings of the engineering test pilots, gathered up during the design, testing, and certification of that airplane. As each plane comes off the assembly line a production test pilot flies it "to make sure it will do what the book says it will do." The owner's manual is a *Federal Aviation Authority* (FAA) approved document, a carefully written work intended to serve you, and sometimes brought into courtrooms as evidence during accident litigation.

The book stays with the airplane, but a good FBO will have low-cost copies of it available to you. Buy one and spend a night with it before you spend too many days with the airplane.

If he is serious, the instructor will invite you to sit in the left seat, traditionally the throne of the *pilot in command*, but in *dual instruction*, the teacher rides right seat. Let him tell you how to close the door. Different planes latch in different ways.

Watch as he goes down his *check list*. All well managed airplanes have a printed check list handy as a reminder of engine start-up and all the other procedures before takeoff. There is another section of it for pre-landing and shutdown. Pilots do not use a check list because they are incapable of remembering these basics; they use it to reinforce their memory. If you ever make a takeoff with the uneasy feeling that you have forgotten something, you probably have. And you probably did not use your check list that time.

Light aircraft have a simple key-turn starter, but unlike autos, they are never "out of gear" when the engine is running. First your instructor will set the brakes, which are activated by toe pressure on top of the *rudder pedals* in modern trainers. The engine bangs smartly to life but seems to be running rough and full of vibrations as compared to an idling car. Part of that is the natural vibrations of the small, four-cylinder, air-cooled power plants that all trainers now have, and part of it comes from the propeller biting the air—the *prop blast*, blowing back along the *fuselage*, and strumming its *tail surfaces*. All of this smooths out and takes on a very reassuring blend of touch and sound once the airplane gets into the element it is designed for: the air.

Airplanes waddle ungracefully and slowly across the ground. What we have here is a tricycle about thirty feet wide being steered by its *nose wheel*. The *rudder* and nose wheel are linked together in most trainers to facilitate ground steering, but sharp turns are made by holding one brake. Aircraft brakes operate independently of each other with enough holding power in the braking system to maneuver out of tight parking places on the *ramp* by locking the brake on one *main wheel* and pivoting the airplane right around it.

Sometimes on the demonstration ride your instructor will let you taxi the airplane out, telling you how to get used to this odd manner of ground steering with your feet.

Watch how your instructor's head swivels, always looking from side to side as you taxi out. Same thing later in flight. He's not nervous or restless, he's careful. Aircraft operate in a see-and-be-seen environment. The silk scarf at the neck of World War I fighter pilots was not altogether a romantic affectation. Tucked into the top of the heavy leather flying coat, the scarf held body heat in and served as a smooth neck bearing for those pilots in open cockpits who stayed alive by searching the skies. We are indoors in a heated cabin now, and Richthofen's Fokker is not about to pounce on us, but pilot neck-swiveling goes on just the same. A midair collision can spoil your whole day.

You will be flying out of one of two kinds of airports. The larger, busier ones are *controlled airports*, characterized by a *control tower*, within which an *Air Traffic Controller* (ATC) directs the flow of traffic by two-way radio. The busiest of these also use radar to visualize and manage the flow of aircraft. At a controlled airport the pilot will be on the radio before he ever moves the plane, and still on it through various changing frequencies until it's finally parked again.

In the order of their usage, the most common radio frequencies from a controlled airport are:

1. *Ground control*—visual direction from the tower to aircraft and vehicles moving on the ground.
2. *Tower*—visual control from the tower of aircraft landing or taking off.

3. *Approach control*—two-way radio or radar control of traffic approaching or departing from the airport, usually within a radius of about 15 to 20 miles of the airport.

4. *Enroute control*—the separation of aircraft on *cross-country* flights, mostly done by radar today. Also called *center*, enroute controllers give traffic and sometimes weather advisories to both IFR and VFR traffic.

5. *Flight service stations* (FSS)—not usually involved in traffic controlling, but on call to all pilots for detailed weather updating and for the airborne filing or amending of *flight plans*.

Aeronautical charts show an *Airport Traffic Area* around each airport that has an operating control tower. This is a 5-mile circle, extending upward to 3,000 feet above ground level (AGL). *Control Zones*, or *Terminal Control Areas* (TCA), are larger areas of airport control with shapes that vary to meet the needs of the locale. *Continental Control Area* is everything above 14,500 feet above *mean sea level* (MSL). *Uncontrolled airspace* is what's left, unless otherwise restricted and shown as such on the charts.

Your first impression may be that flying is mostly aeronautical chart reading, radio talking, and frequency changing. You are partly right, but don't let this put you off. In aviation, as in driving, things get more tranquil as you get farther out into the countryside. Student training is done in a designated remote *practice area* where they leave you pretty much alone.

If you begin flying from a smaller rural airport you will find no control tower, no *controlled airspace*, no radio. Many small fields have a *UNICOM* frequency that pilots share in a kind of a "Hey, Joe" atmosphere.

At both a controlled and non-controlled airport your pilot will stop before he moves out onto the *active runway* and perform his last-minute rituals of the *run-up*:

A. Ground Level
B. Control Tower
C. Airport Traffic Area (5 miles wide, 3,000 feet high)
D. Climb Corridor
E. Federal Airway (8 miles wide, 1,200 up to 18,000 feet)
F. Control Zone or Terminal Control Area (TCA)
G. Restricted Military Operational Area (MOA)
X. Uncontrolled Airspace
H. Continental Control Area (14,500 feet)
I. Positive Control Area (18,000 feet)
J. God

checking the engine under increased power, reading the instruments, moving the controls to see that they are free. When he is through with this last part of the check list and satisfied that the airplane is ready for flight, he will tell the tower: "Two-seven November, ready at three zero."

The first part of that is his radio call sign taken from the last three digits of the registration number of the plane, and the second part is the number of the active runway.

Runways are numbered according to their *magnetic compass* heading, minus the last digit. An airplane lined up on runway three zero will have a compass reading of 300. The other end of the runway would bear the *reciprocal heading* of 120 degrees and go by the family name of runway one two. Runway numbers are painted at the *threshold* of each runway in numbers as big as will fit.

Once the tower has said, "Cleared for takeoff," your pilot will probably take one last look up the *approach* end of the runway to see for himself that no inbound aircraft are about to land, and take a look down the runway to be sure it is all clear.

At a non-controlled airport he will most surely do this because the traffic is self-directed, but even with the tower's OK to go the pilot still looks. No matter what tower or anyone else tells him, he is *pilot in command.* Like a ship captain at sea, and for exactly the same reason, the pilot in command has total authority because he is also totally responsible.

The pilot can override ground controllers. "Not able" can be sufficient reply. But when he returns to earth, and the FAA sends for him as his mother once did, he'd better have a good solid reason for that "not able."

For as long as your instructor flies beside you he is

pilot in command, but once alone, even as a student, you will be the *PIC*.

With the airplane lined up along the centerline of the runway, the pilot now slowly opens the *throttle*. The airplane is going to make the most noise it ever makes during this full-power takeoff.

There is no neck-snapping acceleration, just a steady, powerful gaining of speed. When the plane reaches *flying speed* your pilot will gently ease back the *control wheel*, or *yoke* as it's just as often called, and the airplane will lift off and begin a gentle climb.

This instant, this first sensation of flight as the ground drops away below, is one of those enchanted moments that has hooked so many of us into flying. There is the rush, the feeling of the wings growing fat with *lift*, the plane responsive and eager to fly. There have been times like these when I have felt that the wings sprouted right out of my shoulders. Takeoff is a moment of elation.

Your pilot will reduce the throttle setting from 100 percent takeoff power to the still-strong climb power shortly after takeoff. At a controlled airport he will receive *vectors*, directions to turn and fly in, and continue to climb. The nose of the plane is slightly above the horizon in a climb, and in a turn the earth seems to turn. The horizon line tips and things below come sliding around into your view.

At *cruising altitude*—3,000 or 4,000 feet for demo rides or instructional flights—the pilot will reduce power again, bringing the nose down level with the horizon, and the engine will quiet down. In level flight today's trainers will cruise at a little over 100 miles per hour, but there is no sensation of speed. That's because there is nothing to compare your speed to. You are aloft, distant, as if suspended, and there's no onrushing traffic or blurred telephone poles whipping by. At first only reading the *airspeed indicator* will give you any idea of how fast you are flying. Later you will be able to sense the speed by many subtle things—the sound of the slip-stream, the feel of the controls.

Your first view of the world from the cockpit of a small plane is sort of like meeting a woman for the first time with only her facial expressions to guide you. Later you will know more of where you are with her even if you can't see her face—by the way her heels hit the floor, by the way she sets her coffee cup down.

It is usually along in here that your pilot will invite you to have a go at flying the plane yourself. As with the lady, don't grab or do anything too suddenly.

The pilot probably has been holding the yoke by his finger tips. You do the same. Later you'll find yourself grabbing fistfuls of it. If you ever look down at your hands and see white knuckles, it's time to turn loose a minute, take a few deep breaths, flex your fingers some. Airplanes are to be held like scrolls, not hammers.

Your pilot may show you how to do some gentle banking turns and climbs. You'll find the control motions are almost natural. He should show you the designed stability built into modern trainers: hands off, they tend to seek straight and level flight by themselves.

You probably won't have the feeling of teetering height that one gets when peering down from a tall building. The cabin of the plane seems to be an intact solid and reassuring little world of its own. And if this is a good demo flight you won't come away from it over-whelmed at the idea that you have committed yourself to learning to manage this small island in the sky all by yourself.

Aside from the beauty of it, the sense of grace and motion, the view, the feeling of freedom and of having exercised some new power and control over your own hitherto ground-bound existence, flying can be a very bumpy ride. Doesn't seem like it should be, planing through nothing but air like that, but the air can be rough at times. There are no such things as "air pockets." That is a misnomer left over from the early and unknowing days of flight. There are downdrafts and updrafts, but the nearest you will ever come to an air pocket will be the air left in your pockets after you have paid for the experience of flight.

But if your first ride is on a hot summer midafternoon the plane will slam, bang, thud, rise, fall, in a constant restless manner, as it travels through this smooth and empty-looking air. This light turbulence is caused by unevenly heated columns of air rising from the ground. Called *convection currents*, they bob and joggle your wings. No mystery here. Plowed ground, sand, rock, and barren soil tend to reflect more rising heat than water, vegetation and forests.

Above the usual low level of scattered summer clouds the air is cooler and deliciously smooth and undisturbed as it is in early-morning, late-afternoon, and night flight. Something to know if you are troubled with motion sickness at first.

Popping a motion-sickness pill is OK if you are only going as a passenger, but any over-the-counter or prescription drug that induces drowsiness, as these often do, is something that even the boldest of us eagles avoid as pilots.

Persistent airsickness really did discourage and embarrass me at first. For a while I brought a small bucket and flew with it between my knees. Once I actually began to pilot the plane I was never troubled again. But I can still get "mal-de-air" riding as a passenger, especially in the back seat. I can find relief by tipping my head back as far as it will go; I try for horizontal, close my eyes, and put my mind far away. Once on the ground a cold 7-Up is the best stomach settler for me.

And finally, airsickness ain't funny, although you may be the only person who believes this at the time. There is also a really mean old aviation tradition about who cleans up the airplane.

Wishing you a happy belly on your demo ride, let's head for "homeplate," as the Navy calls it. Don't feel embarrassed if you feel turned around even over your own home town and can't find the direction back to the airport. That happened to all of us, too. The scratchings of man not only form fascinating patterns on the face of this earth, but they do look different from the air. And I have yet to get tired of the experience of just flying along, looking out the window at it all.

As your pilot nears the airport he will enter into a standardized rectangular course called the *approach pattern*. With reduced power the engine will idle, the airplane will go into a *glide*, and don't be alarmed when the pilot turns to you and casually says, "We are on final approach." This does not mean all is lost. *Final approach* is just the standard term for the glide toward the runway that ends in the delicate curving out of the descent just over the runway and the gentle rolling of the wheels on this large turning ball in space called earth. You have returned.

If you still feel good about flying, here is what you can expect in terms of your student hours that lie ahead. For most people, at somewhere around ten hours of dual instructions your pilot will casually step out of the airplane and ask you to take it around by yourself a couple of times. This unforgettable moment is your first *solo*.

There is a contradiction of terms here. As a brand-new solo student, a fledgling barely able to fly from the nest, you will quickly be set free on your student solo flight where technically you are pilot in command.

You will not really be a "pilot" yet. Though some students require more, the regulations require that you fly

thirty-five to forty hours minimum before you are qualified to fly with the examiner for your private pilot's
check ride. Of this time, half will be more dual instruction and learning navigation, *cross-country* flying, a little
bit of instrument flying and night flying. You will learn
to use radio navigational aids, study aviation weather,
and practice emergency procedures. By the time your
instructor is ready to sign you off to the Federal Aviation Administration flight examiner he will be as satisfied as you are that you are ready. The private pilot's
exam consists of two parts, a written exam and a flight
test. Studying for the written test should be proceeding
parallel to your increasing flying experience.

One of the best parts of learning to fly will be the
early hands-on experience which begins in the first hour
and the mystic first solo which seems to come so soon.
It's a kind of a stunt, but not an uncommon one, that
some airstruck kid, upon reaching his minimum qualify-
ing age of sixteen years, will go out on his birthday, start
early and fly all day and solo on the same day.

Whether you are sixteen, sixty, or older, there is no
upper age limit to flying as long as you are fit enough to
pass a rather basic medical examination. I know of two
flight instructors who are both in their eighties and both
still active, and I have at least one friend who passed his
private pilot's exam and became eligible for Medicare
the same day. I know of several women who, having
raised their families and stared without enthusiasm into
a future of gin-and-tonics and bridge games, sallied
forth to the airport to find out if grandmas can be taught
to fly. Yes. And the experience would have to rank
higher than being a halfway good Sunday painter in
terms of discovering new beauty and a sense of satisfac-
tion in your life.

It is a great asset among couples if the flying experience is at least shared at the language level if not in

actual flying. One of the two is going to be coming home just bursting with enthusiasm and stories to tell for too long. One foot flying and one foot dragging can be a strain. In my joyful travels as a speaker for aviation, one of the most common questions, nearly always asked from the audience when the wife is there, is this: "I love flying. It has become a rich and fulfilling part of my life, but now that I'm a private pilot and my wife could go with me, she won't. She says flying gives her a sick headache. Anything you can say to us?"

I always tell them the same thing. I say, "My first wife used to feel the same way about it."

In my own enthusiasm here, don't let me give you a target-date fixation on "ten hours to solo, forty hours to private pilot exam." Those are only point-of-reference numbers. Students have soloed in as few as five hours, or more than fifteen. There are no fixed rules. When your instructor believes you can safely solo, he'll let you do it.

In those first hours of dual instruction the basics of flying will be easier done than they are told here in words. You can "fly"—that is, gently steer the plane where you want it to go—within the first hour or two.

From the beginning you will be taught to recognize a *stall* and how to cope with one. A stall begins when an airplane does not have enough airspeed for its flight conditions. One of my early instructors, Alfred Grant Vanneman, used to say, "I don't like stalls and the airplane doesn't either."

An ordinary, straight-ahead stall is recognized by the airplane slowing down, nose high, controls sluggish, a little shuddering as the wings lose their lift, and the loud honking of the stall warning horn in the cockpit. The cure for any stall is always the same: shove the yoke forward. Please don't ever forget that.

Practice stalls, done at altitude, are not hazardous, and learning to sense the approach of a stall is most valuable. Mastering the basics of stalls and recovery will not fill up an hour. The technique of landings and take-offs will fill up nearly all your dual instruction time before solo.

You should be taxiing out and doing fairly decent takeoffs within the first hours of dual instruction. Exploring stalls will quickly remove the mask of the unknown from that fundamental part of flying safely, but landings just take us all longer to learn. There are more variables to landing. They will require a more subtle touch and technique than you will have at first. Even some professional pilots are content with a sort of "ker-whump" arrival, but to me landings are still the most interesting part of flying, and although I was a slow learner (much to the exasperation of my mentors), I still see each new landing as a sort of challenge to feather it on better than I have ever done it before. I still get a lot of "ker-whumps," too. Sometimes, tired at the end of a long day's journey, I'll thud my airplane in and as I open the throttle to go around and do it again I'm saying to myself, "Hell, I'm not going to let this fine trip end like that."

Part of this is echoes from long-departed instructors; their voices I hear yet. Since the instructor is going to be such a vital link between you and the airplane, the person you hire to teach you how to fly becomes important. Let us speak of flight instructors. They are not all the same.

IF YOU SCARE ME,
I'M GOING HOME

Your instructor will open the skies to you, so find one that you feel good with. By the very nature of the FAA requirements a *Certified Flight Instructor* has got to be good at it, but learning to fly is also a human experience. It will help a lot if you like and respect that fellow human who will be sitting beside you, inches away, mingling sweat and emotions in the crowded cockpit of a little training plane on a hot summer day.

No matter how you cloak yourself in the outside world, in the airplane you and your instructor will come to see each other's naked souls. He will come to know all your secret sins and weaknesses, as well as your inner strengths, and should always be trying to bring out the best in you.

Statistically, teaching flying is not especially dangerous, yet your instructor must let you go as deep as he dares into some risky-looking flying in order for you to learn and make the corrections yourself. He's sitting there beside you, looking calm, but ever ready to snatch you both out of danger. The outcry "If you scare me, I'm going home" did not come from a student. It came from an instructor.

My partner in flying is a *Certified Flight Instructor, Instrument* (CFII). His name is Elmer Lee Ashcraft, and along with his wife, Elaine, who is also a pilot, our pride is a pampered 1968 model *Mooney* Ranger. This swift and sharp little time machine gets the unblushing plug of being the role model here. When we must use some airplane's N-number as a radio call sign example, it's N 6727 November. Our own baby. Elmer Lee teaches the exacting science of instrument flying in 27 November, and his philosophy of teaching is worth telling. It is also typical. I'm sure he adopted it from the long line of instructors before him.

"So much of flying is the development of good habit patterns. A good instructor will not go on to something else until the two of you are satisfied that you have mastered doing it the right way. I never let a student finish it wrong," says CFII Ashcraft.

A final appropriate comment on flight instruction comes from the 20/20 hindsight of a private pilot who demolished his airplane and survived the crash during his early years of private flying. "There is nothing wrong with the amount of training that pilots are getting. The important thing is for pilots to do the things they already know they are supposed to do."

With a little luck you'll get a flight instructor whose voice you will hear as long as you fly. What you need to know now is that if you don't feel good with your instructor you can get a different one.

I can think of no other relationship quite like that of the flying student and instructor. There is an immediate conflict of the lines of authority. In terms of a simple transaction, you have hired the instructor and he is working for you. As the one who is paying the bill you have the right to question and have some voice in determining the sequence of events. Yet by federal law he is the pilot in command and is solely responsible for your safety and his own. One of the touchiest things in learning to fly is to know when to override your instructor.

Being a flight instructor is one of the quickest and most affordable means of amassing great numbers of hours of flying time. And all the really good flying jobs require that the applicant have great numbers of flying hours. Lots of experience. Teaching flying is unquestionably experience.

So the flight instructor is most often a person still in his early twenties who is building up hours in the time-honored way of teaching flying on his way up to the greater glory of being a corporate or airline pilot.

The student, by contrast, is often a person who has reached middle years and is successful enough at whatever he's doing to be able to afford flying lessons.

It would not be out of the ordinary for the president of a small firm to find himself under the command of one of his shipping clerks who is moonlighting as a flight instructor. Now, there is a special air of idealized democracy that begins the minute you set foot across the border of any airport. The common interest in airplanes somehow makes who you are on the other side of the airport fence unimportant. The doctor and the auto mechanic lie down as lambs and lions in the shade of the wing of an airplane and idle away precious hours talking flying. The mechanic doesn't remember how long he has sat in the doctor's waiting room, and the doctor doesn't remember how long the mechanic has kept his car immobile.

Yet there is a little estrangement on the parts of both parties when the twenty-two-year-old flight instructor yells at his forty-two-year-old executive student, "Get the nose up! How many times do I have to tell you to get that nose up? . . . sir."

A few words about yelling in the airplane. Because of the din, a raised voice is the only way to be heard. Because of this some say the airplane cabin is a poor classroom. Actually the airplane is its own best class-room for teaching you the touch of flying, but it's no place to lecture or take notes. A good instructor should spend some pre-flight time with you, talking about what is going to happen and what is to be expected in the coming flight. Most instructors do this, or will if asked. Then the flying can proceed with only a nudge from his set of controls, or a gesture, a frown, a raised eyebrow, or a few clear meaningful phrases.

Also ask your instructor to spend at least a little de-briefing time with you afterward to tell you how it went. Surprisingly few will do that; they nearly always have something they just have to do next, and you're nearly always busting to talk about that last landing. Tell him when you hire him that you want at least a few words afterward. I never got it, and I missed it. The very fact that we went on to something else seemed to be answer enough that I was learning. But how good was I?

Nobody ever told me. I had flown for some years and was taking the check ride with the examiner for my *commercial ticket* test before I ever got a hint. Jerry Griffin, who had flown with me back in those early days and was then the FAA examiner, said, "Baxter, I'm sure glad to see you get this commercial ticket. The instruc-tion has really cleaned up your flying. You always had the most natural feel for an airplane and were at the same time the sloppiest pilot I ever saw." Somehow that meant a lot to me.

There are some instructors who get worked up and yell at you in a manner of steady harassment. Most of these guys are left over from World War II. This is called "stress teaching," and it was the style back then. The abuse resembles the old frat-house hazing concept, and has the same roots. Back when aviators were a small daring band of the elite the thinking was: "You cannot possibly understand my art. But since you dare to approach us, then you must first suffer." This scenario ends with you earning your silver wings at last and being allowed to stand up at the bar and drink with real pilots.

Baloney.

Few personalities are suited to learn best under stress. Unless you are one of these, go hire another instructor.

Ole-timey stress teaching

There is some justifiable yelling in an airplane. One of these times is knowing when to yell, "You got it!" In dual-control flying your instructor will at first help you through his set of controls. He may say, "Now follow me through." Later, especially in learning to land, he may override you on the controls to ease you out of an awkward situation.

As you get better it will be harder to detect if he helped or not, but you may come to depend on his rescuing you at the last minute. Then on some really hard landing bounce you'll relax, just sitting there waiting for him to take over, and that may be the very time he's made up his mind that you are good enough to solve this one by yourself. What we would have there for an instant would be an airplane at the apogee of a graceful high bounce and nobody flying it. Anytime you want to give up on the try, make sure the instructor hears you say, "You got it!"

The idea that there could be uncertainties as to who is actually flying the plane may sound ridiculous, but it happens, and not just to students. Two experienced aviators were once fished, red-faced, out of the Pacific Ocean because they allowed their expensive airplane to coast right down into the drink. Each one thought the other "had it" and was just playing "chicken."

Old friends, recalling those summer evenings when I was learning to fly the old *Aeronca*, claimed they could hear my "You got it!" through the open window and clear across the airport. And they add that my voice came in a high, girlish soprano.

My instructor in those first hours of flight was Ray Gannaway. And Gannaway was a good example of a non-stress teacher.

In the little old-fashioned Aeronca the *carburetor heat* control knob perched on the window sill halfway between our fore-and-aft seats. Then, as now, the carburetor heat should be on when the power is reduced for the landing glide. I was so caught up in more serious things, like aiming it at the runway, that I forgot the carburetor heat.

Gannaway leaned forward and said it in my ear, and I reached back and set the knob. Later we reduced this to where a tap on the shoulder would serve to remind me. Still later he began to appeal to my better instincts and pride. Still I forgot sometimes.

Once, with an approach calmed down enough to ransack my mind for things I had forgotten, I remembered the carb heat and reached for it in a flash. Groping back, I was surprised to feel it in the "on" position. Turning to look and be sure, my eyes met the mild blue eyes of Gannaway. He was sitting well back in the seat, relaxed, arms folded across his chest, smiling at me like a pixie.

Many years, many thousands of miles have gone under my wings. In faraway places I reach for the carb heat now and I see the ghost of Gannaway's smile.

There is a lot of that to come to you in flying. That and their dear little phrases. Gannaway cured me of not looking first before a turn by wryly observing that even a goose does. They do, too.

Even a goose looks before he turns.

The instructors, the small early incidents, will come back like old photos in a family album. Gannaway was an example of the older men you still find teaching flying. A World War II fighter pilot, he was then employed as a *flight controller* in the tower at the Beaumont–Port Arthur, Texas, airport. He moonlighted as a flight instructor both for the extra income and to keep his hand in as a pilot. He liked it.

But what of these younger flight instructors? And what of these graying moonlighters? How good are they?

This is one of the few times you can be glad for lots of U. S. Government intervention. Your certified flight instructor holds one of the hardest-won and most respected of the many grades of flying certificates. He gets examined, inspected, and reinspected more often than fresh pork.

Even if he seems to be just a youngster and you are his first student, his minimum requirements are that he must be at least eighteen years of age with at least 250 hours of flying time and be rated as both a commercial pilot and *instrument pilot.* Just getting all that together can be an intense little career in itself.

He will also have passed both oral and written examinations on the study of the learning process in humans, the elements of effective teaching, student evaluation and testing, course planning and classroom techniques. And in actual flight conditions he had to demonstrate a quick hand and eye for detecting and correcting the errors of a student pilot in flight.

Your instructor must keep a written and signed log of all that happens between you and him. And he will also start the log book of your flying history and later give it to you. In your crackly-clean log book he will enter a laconic description of what the two of you did that day. All of these notations go into the book over his own signature and his cherished certificate number.

A good set of rules have evolved to protect both you and him and to keep the level of instruction high and fairly uniform. Every two years all of his certificates to fly and to teach flying will come up for review, and he must show an FAA examiner that he can do all that he is licensed to do. And there are also controls over this system of controls. The FAA examiner who examines the instructor must have proof of his own current proficiency from the examiner who examined him.

Your flight instructor must be in good health. Each year he must stand before a medical examiner and pass a physical examination, and he is forbidden to teach more than eight out of twenty-four hours in an airplane.

All of this is just academic if he can't teach people to fly. So if at least 80 percent of his students do not pass their own examination for private pilot he is suspended and hauled in and asked why.

A flying instructor must go through an awful lot to get and keep his certificate, yet if anyone ever got rich just teaching flying I have yet to hear of it.

YOU DON'T HAVE
TO GO TO SCHOOL

The Wright brothers designed their own airplane and taught themselves to fly it. When the Army bought their first flying machine from the Wrights they shipped it down to San Antonio, Texas, where the weather was better than Ohio, and assigned young Lieutenant Benjamin D. Foulois to learn how to fly it. Foulois assembled the thing, which was designed to be transported by wagon, and began to write letters to the Wrights back in Dayton about how to fly. All this worked out better than you'd think. The military still teaches flying in sunny San Antonio, and Foulois became the commanding general of the Air Corps.

Lindbergh bought a few flying lessons, then went to Souther Field, Georgia, and paid cash for an old war-surplus *Jenny*. A more experienced pilot, also there to buy a Jenny, observed young Lindbergh bouncing and skittering across the turf and tactfully offered him a little dual instruction. Lindbergh accepted, then flew away home, crashing and learning more as he went.

This took place in the early 1920s. Later in that decade, Oscar Meyer, of Hendersonville, South Carolina, designed and built himself an airplane because there was no other way he could get one, and taught himself to fly it because nobody would risk going up with him in the Model A Ford–powered crate. Then he began to teach flying and take passengers up for hire because there was no other way to support an airplane.

He had founded the airport at Hendersonville and was a successful FBO when, as he tells it, "one day in the '30s an inspector found his way into my valley and I let myself get under the thumb of the government. He just walked down the flight line and licensed all my airplanes, then told me to go up and show him a few turns and a *spin* or two. It was a cold day. He stayed inside by the stove. He licensed me when I came down."

Today there are formal flight schools at most airports, and four-year degree courses in aviation careers are offered at many universities, but even now, you don't *have* to go to school to learn how to fly. The good old master-apprentice relationship is still an option open to you, even as it was in the beginning.

I learned to fly in this manner. Not as a matter of choice, but because there were no real flying schools in my part of Texas in those days. I enjoyed the freedom of it, the independence of study at home and the come-and-go, fly-when-you-can-afford-it, casual way of it all. There were disadvantages to this, but I was unaware of them because I had nothing to compare it to. I attended no *ground school*, and my knowledge of the theory of flight, study of weather, and the Federal Air Regulations was absolutely minimal. And I have been playing catch-up ever since.

I just got up the nerve to go out to the airport one afternoon, walked into the pilots' service building, and asked the line foreman at the desk that classic question, "Who do I see around here to take flying lessons?"

The man was bored, but friendly. He said Ray Gannaway took students part-time, and told me how to find Gannaway over at the tower. Gannaway didn't laugh out loud at the idea or ask me to do pushups on the cement. He was a mild, graying little fellow who just took me out to the airplane and said let's get in, as if this were the most everyday thing in the world and not an event I had been fantasizing about since I was sixteen years old, building model airplanes, and had first seen the movie *Men with Wings*.

The little Aeronca was affectionately called the *Rag Doll* because of its yellow fabric covering, which hung sort of loose and soft with age. To me, then, it looked and smelled like the most serious airplane in the world.

Gannaway showed me how to open the door, get in, and set the brakes for him. By hand he gave the propeller a sort of casual flip and the engine began to run, making mild, buttery sounds. Then we flew away. It was as simple as that.

This manner of learning to fly is still open to the applicant. The requirements are detailed in a government publication called *Federal Aviation Regulations for Pilots*. This inexpensive paperback is available at most FBO offices. You should have it.

A complete set of the bound copies of all the FARs would be more than a man could carry in both arms, but this booklet has within it the two parts of the FARs that you need to be familiar with. My partner, Ashcraft, described these two parts best: "Part 61 tells you how to get your license. Part 91 tells you how to keep it." Part 61 is the requirements for pilot certification and ratings. Part 91 is the general operating flight rules.

Learning to fly in the traditional, self-directed manner

is called a Part 61 flight course. A postwar development in flight instruction is the more tightly controlled Part 141 flight school.

The Part 141, also called a Certified Flight School, came along with the GI Bill. It was almost as if the government had said, "OK, if we are going to pay your way to learning to fly we are going to exercise some control over the matter."

Part 141 Certified Flight Schools are not necessarily connected to the GI Bill any longer, but with their prescribed hours of ground-school curriculum nearly all of the bigger FBOs and full-time flight schools are Part 141 Certified Flight Schools with full-time professional instructors.

Let's compare the advantages and disadvantages of Part 61 and Part 141 flight training.

In the small-town, small-airport, Part 61 manner of learning to fly, you can be a part-time student. But your instructor may be part-time too. You could come out to the airport all psyched up to fly and find that he had to work overtime at his regular job and left you a note to come back another day. Or if both of you manage to get out to the airport together you may find that the only available training plane, which he is renting from somebody else, is broken down and can't fly. Or that there was a mix-up in the plans and some other son of a gun has flown off in it for the day. You will often as not trek back home, unflown.

You will also find that the home-study course is a mindbender. The self-teaching approach to the ground-school knowledge that you will need to pass the written part of the private pilot's exam requires a lot of self-discipline.

A Part 61 student is eligible for the flight test after a minimum of forty hours of student flying time. The Part 141 student, better trained (it is assumed) by his Certified Flight School, is eligible for the flight test after only thirty-five hours.

Don't be overly impressed by these minimum hour requirements and set them as your goal. Most of us in aviation today feel that is just barely enough training. Get all you can. It took me about forty-five hours as a student in my haphazard approach to learning to fly, and looking back now I wouldn't have gotten into an airplane with me then for a million bucks.

Yet if because of your remote location or your own independent persuasion you do choose the self-directed manner of learning to fly, don't let me give you the impression that you will be a lesser pilot. When you sit down at the table to take the written examination there is no question about how you got there. And in that flight test the examiner will only care about how good you are, not where you learned.

There are many valuable books in print which will teach you what you need to know to pass the written exam. My own favorite is the least expensive and, oddly enough, is a government publication. It's the precisely written and clearly illustrated *Pilot's Handbook of Aeronautical Knowledge*, and like the booklet of FARs, it is commonly available at the FBO's showcase. The *Pilot's Handbook* covers the basic subject of becoming a private pilot.

With the *Pilot's Handbook*, purchase the companion piece—the government-published *Private Pilot's Airplane Written Test Guide*. This one has about 600 questions in it, along with the correct answers. Sixty of these questions are exactly what you will face when you go to take the written test.

What makes these two books such a workable combination for home study is that you won't know which of those questions and answers will be in the constantly changing test. By making you study them all, the FAA, which produced both books, can be pretty sure you will have to learn all the things it wants you to know.

The late Bob Marsh, who used to run a good flight school at Houston, once gave me some wry and apt advice on passing the FAA written exams. March said, "I am going to teach you to do two things here. I am going to teach you to safely pass the flying part of this test, and I am going to teach you to pass the written part of this test. These are related matters, but not the same thing."

I was preparing for my instrument flying rating, and Bob was preparing me for the confrontation with the government written exam, which is one of the most cussed and exasperating of all federal printed matter, with the possible exception of income tax forms.

The FARs, and the FAA written tests, are written in governmentese, a language I sometimes think was invented to obscure meaning. In times of sweating and teeth-grinding frustration, bent over these pages, I have often guessed that it was all written by lawyers, not aviators, and that none of it was intended to support an airplane in flight but rather to support a case in court.

Bob Marsh, an old gray pelican who flew thousands of hours as a Navy patrol boat pilot during the war, said, "The trouble with you is that you are a wise guy. A speed reader. You gulp paragraphs, thinking you already know their meaning. Now, you do these Mickey Mouse things I am about to show you."

And he made me tear off a strip of paper, cover all the paragraph but the top line with it, and move the paper down as I read the matter line by line, lips moving. It works.

His other sage advice had to do with the written exam's form, which now is the same on all FAA tests. "It's a four-part multiple-choice question. The correct answer is one of the four, sitting right there looking at you. On a scratch pad, number down the page a line for each question. Across the pad, draw four columns, numbering them one through four, for the four multiple-choice answers. Now you have a gridded space to write in for each answer on each question. The code letter you will write in that space will be P or O. That stands for 'possible' or 'out.'

"Those four answers are made up of two obviously wrong ones, the right one, and a 'deceiver.' That's the one you gotta look out for. It sounds like a correct answer, but has some small buried flaw in it. Key words that flag a deceiver are 'must' and 'always.' Very few of the FARs are written like that. But they will use other ways of writing a good deceiver too.

"As soon as you find the two obviously wrong answers, write an 0 in their spaces on your pad. Now you've just got two questions left to seriously consider. You won't keep darting back and considering the out ones, and you have already raised your odds of answering correctly to a fifty-fifty chance. But most important, you have located and separated the true answer and the deceiver so that you can study and compare and concentrate on them."

Before the exam Marsh gave me a dummy test, based on what he knew would be in the real one. Then he offered to bet me two bits he could predict my score. "You will make a 78. And that's OK. Anything over 70 is as good as 100."

I made a 78 and paid the bet with a check for twenty-five cents, which he kept framed and hung up in his office.

At large airports the FBO usually has a pilot training center, a classroom, and a staff of full-time flight instructors built right into the operation. Such a school might be a Part 61 or a Part 141—the difference is hard to find except that if it is a Part 141 Certified Flight School it usually brags about it in its advertising. Part 141 flight schools tend toward classroom instruction; Part 61 schools still include home study.

A Part 141 school will have a small fleet of late-model training planes in good condition, and it will make appointments and keep them. The instructor usually wears a white shirt and dark tie, and you may not get the same one every time.

The office will offer you a "package deal," a contract of some sort within which various means of payment can be arranged. The Part 141 schools usually charge a little more, but explain that you are qualified to finish five hours sooner. Brush this aside; all of it is going to take longer than the idealized proposal. Most will admit that.

In fact, do not let price shopping color your decision on where to learn to fly. It costs more in big cities, just as everything else does, but the price of an instructor and the costs of operating a training plane all go up at about the same rate at the same time all across the country. Let your deciding factors be the more important ones of finding an instructor and an environment that you feel easy with.

One reason for the sameness in price, which is pretty close to cost, is that it's competitive. There just never have been enough students to go around. And although there never has been much advertising or promotion about learning to fly, student instruction is the very foundation of the whole world of aviation. It also shows the lowest profit yield of anything the FBO does. The money is in selling airplanes and selling gasoline.

It is surprising to me that the aircraft manufacturers themselves have only recently gotten involved in student training as a part of the strategy for selling airplanes. Traditionally, the new airplane was a sort of holy object and you came and got one when you were at last worthy of it.

Piper and *Cessna*, the Ford and Chevy of airplane makers, finally developed student training programs operated through their dealers only because of after-market sales. One of them correctly decided that a pilot tends to be loyal to the type of aircraft he first learned to fly in. Therefore a student who learns in a little two-seater Cessna is most likely to stick with Cessna when he's up there buying big two-engined airplanes. And when one manufacturer started a training program, the other quickly followed. So did *Beechcraft*, the Cadillac of light planes.

The factory student training center was a new concept, not an evolutionary classroom outgrowth of the old pilot sitting on the bench and talking earnestly to his student. And in new concepts of education the buzzword is "audiovisual." Factory training comes with more projectors, film, tape, and speakers than a rock band.

Electronic teaching is said by some to be more attuned to the younger generation's TV background of sitting and learning before *Captain Kangaroo*. With admitted older-generation prejudice in my heart, I still prefer to learn by taking notes from a live teacher in a classroom, then going home and surrounding myself with the familiar paraphernalia of textbooks festooned with page-finding slips of paper and pages with key phrases jumping out from under transparent lines from a broad yellow marking pen.

In all fairness, the most advanced aviation training school is the American Airlines Academy near Dallas, where jet pilot training for the most sophisticated airliners, flown by the most well-mannered pilots, is conducted almost entirely in an audiovisual environment. Even the pilot of the President's *Air Force One* goes there.

Some FBOs offer Part 61 or Part 141 training at the same place. You can still choose the ground-school or flight-school or no-school environment that suits you best.

Although the FAA examiners will be impartial as to where you learned to fly and how you learned the rules, there is one aspect of where you choose to learn to fly that you will probably carry with you forever. The typical home-study student, flying out of a non-controlled pasture airport, will be ill at ease in the big-city, busy-airport environment. Likewise, the city-bred student will feel disoriented and nervous in his first silent approach to a rural airport with its short, narrow landing strip.

After the first few hours of instruction at the big Beaumont–Port Arthur airport, I did most of the rest of my flying for many years off the clover of little grass fields. The runways were always short and narrow, and at Orange County airport they grew a good sorghum crop right up to the edges, to supplement their meager income from students such as me.

On at least one early landing I buried a runaway airplane in the tall sorghum, suffering no damage except to my pride. No student likes to be called "the harvester," even if he did cut a pretty good swath.

But when we practiced doing a *short-field takeoff* or *soft-field takeoff* we could do it for real. I was taught to swing my rudder around right up against the barbed-wire fence, stand on the brakes and open the throttle until all was a-quiver, then, making a short L-shaped run, slew it around up onto the runway and stagger into the air before we came to the cows.

I learned as a matter of course to fight a strong *cross-wind* and come slipping in over the trees and *sink* it firmly onto the grass and keep it hemmed up on a runway 60 feet wide from cornstalk to cornstalk. Naturally I became sort of proud of this, and always figured that if I had to I could drop an airplane into a football field and not go out of bounds. The light little Aeroncas and *Cubs* of our day would do that. The most worrisome thing in my mind when I thought of the chances of having to make a *forced landing* somewhere someday was how far I would have to walk to get to a phone and whether the farmer's daughter would be beautiful.

But when it came my turn to fly into Houston, to mix in with all that fast, heavy traffic, use the radio and talk to a control tower, and figure out which one of all those long broad cement runways he was talking about, I was terrified. The only traffic I had ever dodged up until this point was a few curious chicken hawks that liked to sail up alongside and look me over. That ain't like having the tower yell at me, "*Break right*, there's a *DC-6* right behind you!"

I landed flustered at big-city airports, and I hate to admit it, but I still do.

In contrast to my pasture-pilot skills is the student who never knew anything but a big, crowded, jet-screaming airport with the tower yakking at him over four frequencies from the time he turns a wheel until he's safely back in the *chocks*. He will grow up street-wise, trafficwise, sharp and crisp on the radio. He doesn't resent his sky being all sliced up into areas and zones and ground people telling him when to turn left, turn right, or blow his nose. He never knew it any other way.

He becomes a good, skillful, and careful pilot—the kind that more and more airports require today. It's only when he's out in the countryside with nobody telling him what to do that he becomes a little uneasy. The sky is free and empty all around him. There is silence on the radio. There is only a *windsock* to tell him which way the wind is blowing and which end of the *airstrip* to land on. And the windsock might have blown away last night.

He's accustomed to seeing clearly marked cement

runways, about 200 feet wide and 7,000 feet long. Now he's staring at grass or a rough humpbacked asphalt strip about 50 feet wide and 2,000 feet long. Where he learned to fly it was customary to let the first 1,000 feet slide under you before you even touched down. If he does that here, he's in real trouble.

It's the old city boy, country boy thing that has always been a part of our culture. The FAA attempts to compensate for this by requiring that the student get a variety of experiences in both kinds of airports. But if you spend your formative hours flying out of pastures and narrow strips you'll always be better at that. And if as a student you get accustomed to being sandwiched in on final approach between a *DC-9* and a *Lear Jet*, it won't bother you nearly as much as when they do that to you the first time.

One other contrast: When the engine starts in a training plane the *Hobbs meter* starts, too. That counts the dollar-hours you fly, in tenths. When you are on the ground at a big airport, waiting, number three to take off, the good old Hobbs thinks you are out there flying. At a grass airport you will be.

The best of all possible worlds would be if you could do your flying out of a small airport that was within kissing distance of a big one.

Up until now we have addressed our discussion of aviation schools toward readers who are established in their careers, and for whom learning to fly will only be a continuing adjunct to their lives and perhaps their businesses as private pilots.

If, however, you are still on the sunny side of thirty and plan to make aviation a full-time career, there are full-time ways of getting professionally qualified for it.

First are the "trade schools," located mostly in the sun-belt states, and all quite reputable. You will never be

Private pilot   Public pilot

ashamed of starting your job-hunting résumé with the name of one of these few good schools. Some trace their beginnings back to the early 1930s when the students built and flew their own wood-and-wire biplanes as a class project.

The trade schools teach the entire spectrum of aviation, from mechanic all the way through to *Airline Transport Pilot*.

A more recent innovation is the full, four-year degree course in aviation now being offered by various universities. If you have any dreams of being an airline captain, you should be aware that this career is so desirable that the way gets very narrow and steep toward the top. The airlines have thousands of applicants at any given time and they just skim the cream.

Nowadays, the airlines are hiring persons under thirty, in the best of physical condition, with a college degree and about 1,000 hours of turbine, or jet-powered, flying time. Unless you have a fine old uncle who can get you into one of the flight-training military academies, getting an aviation degree while logging flying time at college is as good a head start as you can hope for.

These are the expensive and ideal ways to approach that lofty captain's chair on the flight deck of a *B-727*. It is in no way intended to discredit or discourage the *line boy*, out there pumping gas and sweating airplanes into the hangar. The one before him did it: He earned his primary flying time as a line boy, and built hours toward his commercial and *multi-engine* rating as a flight instructor. He got his 1,000 hours jet time pounding along the *commuter* lines, and one day you board a Delta airliner and there he is grinning at you from the co-pilot's seat. "You remember me? I was line boy at Orange County the day you cut that sorghum. How you doing, Harvester?"

And he won't be ashamed of his humble beginnings. After all, that old white-haired guy in the bifocals sitting next to him in the captain's chair started out with Delta dusting cotton.

As in the olden times when a youth could study medicine under a good doctor, or read law in the offices of an old lawyer, and then could sit for his exams when he thought he was ready, you can still do that in aviation. The essential remains unchanged: You've got to want to do it an awful lot.

THE TWO FACES
OF FLYING

In flying there is the "official face," as in textbooks, talking to the press, or to any outsiders, and there is the "other face," the way pilots really talk to each other. The two never mix.

"There are old pilots, and there are bold pilots," we will honestly tell you, "but there are no old bold pilots." We all know this and we believe it.

You will find out, soon after you are among us at the airport, that when any two or more of us gather together we relish telling hair-raising tales of how bold we are; of the dangerous flying we have done, the rules we have bent, and the junky old airplanes we have survived. The stories are great, and they all have the same ending— about how once again we have cheated fate.

From the very beginning, better heads than mine have puzzled over aviation's wonderful schizophrenia; wondered why pilots, already engaged in the unforgiving act of flying, will deliberately take chances and seem to enjoy it—and enjoy the telling of it.

Hearing about the wild stuff that pilots do, and the awful wrecks it gets them into, is highly entertaining. One of the most serious and responsible aviation magazines knows this, and eases their guilt by running such stories as true confessions, or as little morality plays, with all the exciting details still intact, but with a lesson for you at the end. Reader surveys show that it is one of the most popular features of the magazine. It is the only instance I can think of when you will come close to hearing the two faces of aviation speaking from one mouth.

Every strata of aviation is touched by our tendency to have fun with something as serious as flying airplanes. Airline pilots are the best-trained among us. They are the most conservative of men. They set the standards for millions of hours flown safely. You have really got to be in the family to sit in on such stories as the one about the *ferry* crew who *slow-rolled* an empty DC-9. Or of the flat-out, down (on the deck) racing between two competitive airlines that flew the same kinds of planes over the same short route. Or agreeing on the cover-up story after landing at the wrong airport. "We had a fire warning light, and this was only a precautionary landing."

Legendary among line pilots' bar stories is the one about the old captain found napping as his transport plane flew on *autopilot* above solid cloud cover toward a coastline city. His crew reset all of his navigation instruments to read "from" the target city instead of "to." Then they, too, pretended to be asleep and set off the low-fuel warning signal. All this to give the old skipper a few fine moments of awakening to alarms and wondering when he had flown over his destination and how far out over the ocean he was now. They let him sweat a moment before straightening him out. Sure the ole man was mad, but what could he say?

Former airline captain Ernie Gann has flown thousands of safe, scheduled, and uneventful hours, yet his best-selling masterpiece, *Fate Is the Hunter*, is a retelling of those brief moments in his life when everything went wrong, when courage and skill rode supreme and the pilots involved barely escaped with their skins. His dialogue between two pilots meeting on the other side of that "employees only" door is classic:

"Where have you been?"

"Lost, what did you expect?"

"Your personal effects."

Had you met Captain Gann as a passenger you would have met a slight, modest, and highly professional aviator. But ole Gann collected all the great hangar tales, and we loved them. You will notice, however, that he drew the shades down and never fully identified the pilots or the airlines. He couldn't. Because Ernie had let you come into the back of the hangar and listen to the forbidden tales.

As you begin to hear hangar tales you will quickly note that the macho image of the silk-scarf hero pilot is a factor both in the stories and in the accidents. There is plenty of sex in airplanes. In their free movement through the liquid air, in the sensory response of flying them, in the very phallic shape of some of them. You don't have to be a dirty old Freudian reject to look at the long, rounded lines of the Corsair, the Navy's famed World War II fighter plane, and imagine yourself loose in the combat skies over Bali with all that potency and power—fingering life or death with a thumb rubbed against the little red gun button on the joystick. Thirty years after the war, "Pappy" Boynton's story *Baa Baa Black Sheep* still sold, and the TV series of those Corsairs, peeling off into death dives, competed well for a long time against *Charlie's Angels*.

There is plenty of sex in airplanes, but no sexism is

intended in this book when I repeatedly call the instructor "him" or the student "he." Women learn to fly as
easily as men, sometimes better, because so much of
flying is gentle coordination and being able to maintain
a prolonged attention span over small details. The
chances are good and so is your luck if you find a woman
flight instructor. You seldom hear the common com-
plaints of rudeness and impatience from their students.

Women were not particularly welcomed into flying by
men, who preferred to keep the mystique to themselves.
Early women pilots who persisted in pushing themselves
into this male world were regarded even by their own
home-and-hearth sisters as being tinged by the same
faintly racy reputation that is associated with stage
actresses. For what it's worth, all of those early daredevil women pilots were beautiful.

In later years a sisterhood of women pilots was
formed around the memory of Amelia Earhart, best
known of women aviators. The group, called the Ninety-
Nines, is a sort of shelter and supportive organization of
housewives, mothers, and businesswomen who persist in
flying. As a guest speaker at one of the Ninety-Nines'
conventions I stood up and told them that getting used
to seeing women in command of airliners and military
planes was going to take me a little time. But I had no
objection to the idea, and some of my best friends are
women pilots, said I. They took me out onto the patio
and threw me into the pool.

I must admit that the sexual overtones of flying were a
part of the image that attracted me to it. I pictured
myself, helmet and goggles, white scarf and big wristwatch, leaning against the fireplace. Crooked smile, but
even teeth. The only trouble with this was that by the
time I got around to being a pilot, wearing wings had
gone out of style. I still have the old leather jacket and
the big wristwatch, but there were so many of us pilots

lined up against the fireplace that nobody noticed anymore. You'll have to ask your instructor to explain about the legend of the pilot's big wristwatch.

Only in South and Central America can one still find vestiges of the great traditional male-sexist-pig pilot. A few years ago I rode a DC-3 out of Bogotá, Colombia. The pilot was dapper, with a handsome cookie-duster mustache riding his upper lip. He flew low over the jungle, dodging thunderstorms, and somehow locating each little jungle-clearing airstrip with its row of shacks beside the dirt runway. At each clearing, as the dust of his prop wash settled over the storefronts and excited passengers crowded out to meet the plane, a beautiful maiden of the village would come out to him. They would stand and talk softly in the shade of the wing on the offside from all the freight and passenger loading. They talked earnestly, while he nibbled the ice-cream bar she had brought to him. At departure time she would cling to him, pressing her tiptoed body to him in farewell. He seemed to be reassuring her of his faithful and early return. Then he would stroll over a little way, turn his back to her and the passengers watching from the windows, and with care and ceremony, standing there in his blue uniformed coat, he would urinate upon a post. He did this at each of the jungle villages on his schedule. Truly one of the last of a great tradition of airline pilots. Nowadays all you can see them doing in the small terminals of America is eating the ice cream.

There is plenty of sex in airplanes, and in the beginning of airline travel, as now, pretty young women were used as bait. But my wife, a former Braniff hostess, tells me that the real reason for the beautiful stewardesses in the early days when air travel was considered very daring was to "have us stand by that coffin-shaped cabin entry as if to say to all those guys standing there with their knees knocking, 'See, even a little girl can do it.'"

And the legends of the stewardess logging "laptime" with the pilot are true. Although my wife says she sat in the pilot's seat alone instead of in the pilot's lap, she admits that there was nothing so lovely as piloting a huge airliner, boring steadily and smoothly into the velvet night over the Rockies while those trusting souls slept fitfully back there in the cabin, not dreaming that the stewardess might be flying the plane.

An old friend who flies for Eastern tells of one starry night when his co-pilot and the stewardess were logging a little laptime. "I saw a reflection pass over the instruments and realized that the cabin door had silently swung open and all the passengers could see her dangling legs and her curled-up toes. I asked her if she meant to leave the door open and she said she could never go back in the cabin and face all those people ever again."

My wife took her own days as aircrew seriously, but enjoys the stories, as we all do. She resents the sex-kitten image of her former profession. As for her own prudence, she pointed out that any crew base is as gossipy as a small-town party line, and a girl makes and lives with her reputation. But what griped her was this: "All you businessmen looking us up and down as we stand there in the aisle and demonstrate the use of the emergency equipment and tell how to evacuate the cabin. Records of actual crash landings show that those same heroes will sit panic-stricken in their seats in a burning cabin while us 'chicks' direct the evacuation. But that is what we are trained for, and that's one of the real reasons for cabin crews."

Another of the persistent smirks of sex and airplanes is the Mile-High Club. Remaining overnight with a companion in a Denver hotel will not qualify you. Nor, according to Tony Page, will any experience with your mate in any aircraft equipped with an autopilot. Tony is a good example of sex and sexism in aviation. She is a veteran pilot, rated in both airplanes and helicopters, but when she began publishing her little tabloid aviation newspaper, *X-Country News*, Toni changed her name to the masculine spelling Tony for fear that an aviation paper published by a woman would lack credibility in the male world she was a part of.

Sex and airplanes is not all Freudian fantasy, dirty jokes, and subliminal associations with the sensually free movement of planes through the air-ocean. It is also a part of the real-world tendency of the human animal to have some fun.

I have a friend who flies a *Stearman* biplane high over the sunny hills of California with his lady sunbathing in the rear cockpit. And I will admit to a few occasions of nude Mooney flying. On a long solo flight my cabin gets cramped and stuffy and I get bored and clothesbound. So I fly my little plane sans suit. It's as much fun as a skinny-dip in a secluded fresh country creek, up there in the high, cool, clear sunlight. I can't find anything in the Federal Air Regulations that says this is illegal.

Yet, until now, I have been careful about whom I admitted this to. More of the two faces of flying—the stern, moralistic code of behavior that draws a sharp line between the way pilots really do talk and act, and the way we all agree we should talk and act.

All of us, in our official face, deplore the white flying scarf of the hangar tales. The most careful pilot I know is editor of one of the "official" magazines, and he does not write about, or practice, any fooling around in airplanes. Yet he relishes the challenge of flying expertly in really gunky weather. Give him a low icy day that I wouldn't even get out of bed for and he flies—his white scarf secretly streaming.

You can find the two faces of flying among the astronauts, the most tight-lipped, ice-water-for-blood pilots that America has ever produced. In the heyday of our space exploration program the national news reporters complained out loud that they couldn't get anything out of these guys but official Eagle Scout talk. They still can't today. Only in Walt Cunningham's book, *The All American Boys*, did Walt, an astronaut himself, come clean about all the fun you may have suspected that they were having.

In order to maintain their razor edge of skill at flying high-performance aircraft, the astronauts were given access to the T-38 Talon, a supersonic jet fighter-trainer. Cunningham described it as an unbelievably beautiful airplane, and said few women could resist an invitation to come ride in one. Cunningham pointed out that with its faster-than-sound speed, an astronaut could finish up his morning space training at Houston, spend the afternoon visiting with friends out on the West Coast, and be back home in Houston that night. He tells how they played with the airplane. Going out to the coast against the prevailing westerly winds, they had to make a fuel stop at El Paso. Returning to Texas, there was a chance that they could catch strong, favorable tail winds and make it home without stopping. They would crapshoot with the high westward jet stream air currents just for the fun of trying to make it back to Houston nonstop; for the blood-tingling experience of letting it all hang out, as Walt phrased it; for the kick of getting fuel-exhaustion *flame-out* as they turned off the ramp at Houston.

Why this brinkmanship? This streak of madness?

"To put your life in danger from time to time breeds a saneness in dealing with trivialities." That was not uttered by some ace rocket pilot. That was written by Nevil Shute, born 1900, educated at Oxford in science, a distinguished British aircraft designer and noted novelist.

Tom Wolfe also attempted to come to grips with this flyer's combination of courage and foolishness. He borrowed the astronaut's own phrase for it as the title of his book, *The Right Stuff.*

This macho stuff is not always so right. The Navy long ago recognized the trait as a part of what makes a good fighter pilot, but also recognized that such men were high on the accident-prone list. The Navy has tried to channel the daredevil urges with a contempt campaign. They call dangerous, show-off style flying "flat-hatting," and such pilots are known as "Dilberts." The Navy will also take back your golden wings and the little blue box they came in if it can hang reckless flying on you.

Ag pilots are another group of professionals trying to clean up their act, and they must fly low and slow for a living. Their first move was to quit calling themselves "duster pilots," and all of their meetings and publications became unbelievably official and stuffy. Yet the ad men, who are still in touch with what duster pilots are really like, run ads in their own official magazine showing a giant, 1,200-horsepower biplane and call it the Diablo. They show the pilot as a raunchy-looking ace standing spread-legged by the wingtip, helmet, sunglasses, and all, and the copy reads, "Can you handle this devil's challenge?"

The two faces of aviation. We is and we ain't.

Airline pilots not only never talk about their pranks in public, but there is a mysterious cutoff point where they also pretend that none of it ever happens when dealing with each other. In any official business, such as a check ride with each other, they are formal, demanding, and often call each other "Mr." or "Sir."

There is poorly concealed contempt for any pilot who

The two faces of flying

persists in Dilbert-style flying. There seems to be a tolerance for a few blunders now and then, but if this turns out to be your pattern of flying, your hangar stories will start to be shunned. Here, in descending order, are the basic top ten hangar tales and the degree of their social acceptance.

1. Wild landings or takeoffs.
2. Dealing heroically with in-flight mechanical failures.
3. Getting lost and finding your way home.
4. Getting lost and not finding your way home.

5. Buzzing your loved one's house.

6. Running out of gas.

7. A crash you can walk away from.

8. Flying into bad weather.

9. Flying while drinking or doping. (NOTE: If your crowd accepts this, change crowds. Either is a serious taboo.)

10. Getting killed in a crash.

You will notice that all classic hangar tales deal with survival. If you have the misfortune to be killed in an airplane, your story will go around just once. Then you, and the event that carried you away, will never be mentioned again.

Hangar flying can be instructional. We learn from the other guy's misfortunes. We have often joked that the time spent listening to these tales should be allowed in the student pilot's logbook. Maybe at only 50 percent value, since at least half of it is lies.

But the other-face-of-flying stories can be much more gripping to hear and easier to remember than the lessons from the pedantic teachings of the official face. Here is an example.

Making low and slow turns while your attention is diverted toward the ground is one of the most hazardous things a pilot can do. And nearly all low-time pilots are bound to go and do it. Once there was a hotshot Stearman pilot who rented one of these grand old biplanes and went off to buzz his girlfriend's house. She lived on a mountainside in North Carolina in a cottage shaded by tall trees. Hearing the mighty roar of her hero's engine, she trotted out and waved prettily from the yard. Swooping by his lady love, doing a low slow turn and waving back to her, the pilot hung his Stearman in one of the tall trees beside her house. The mighty hardwood uprooted with the snared Stearman in its branches. The impact of the airplane uprooted the tree and it all went rolling, shouting, and crashing down the mountainside, making a terrible mess. The wonderful old Stearman was balled up forever, the grand old shade tree was gone, the pilot's girlfriend quit him, and the FBO who had rented the airplane ran him off for good. And this true story is still being told in the mountain country south of Ashville.

Now isn't that more memorable and picturesque than me just trying to tell you that low and slow turns are more dangerous than they appear to be?

As we said in the beginning, unless you are already suffering the comradeship of aviators, do not expect to just drop in at the airport and begin to enjoy the benefits of hangar flying. The chatter among pilots will dry up as soon as a stranger approaches. They may look at you with the innocent eyes of teenagers found in a room full of smoke when nobody appears to be smoking anything.

It is not uncommon to remain on somewhat reserved terms with your instructor during the interim of student flying, or have a dual relationship with his official face in the airplane, and the other face on the ground.

So when, you may rightfully ask, do you get past your new-boy-at-this-club status and become a part of the other face of flying? It will begin the day something happens to you. The day you burst into the pilot's coffee room full of excitement and cry out, "Did you guys see that last landing? That thing must have bounced hangar high. I bet I left permanent dents in that runway!" And they will all laugh and agree that you are probably the most inept student that anyone here can remember.

But this will not be the story you will take home with you that day to tell your folks, who warned you not to take up flying anyway. They would not understand the language or the circumstances, and anyway, you want them to think well of aviation. We are still selling the general public on the idea that flying is a good thing.

So you will suppress all that which is going on inside you. They will ask, "How did flying go today?"

And you will grin at the memory of how it really went today, and officially tell them, "Just fine—we're in the landing syllabus now."

The two faces of flying.

AIRPLANES WILL
DO WHAT THEY
LOOK LIKE
THEY WILL DO

Most student instruction in the postwar years has taken place in light two-seater training planes which are more or less designed for the job. They are basically honest and docile little airplanes. You can look at one sitting there on the ramp and tell that it won't do you any harm. They are as predictable and stable as a well-trained pup; you really have to provoke one to make it bite.

People have learned to fly in all sorts of airplanes, not just the standard trainers that we will describe here. There is nothing in the rules that says what you may learn to fly in, although there are some good common-sense limitations in the FARs that specify what you may not.

"No larger aircraft" is their way of eliminating such obvious planes as jet-powered ones or big aircraft requiring more than one pilot, or airplanes so big or complex as to require separate instruction in that type only. This loose ruling does leave the door open to most of the airplanes found on a general aviation ramp. People have bought complex, fast four-place airplanes or light twin-engined planes and learned to fly in them. But it's better to get started in as simple an airplane as you can find. Once you have acquired the touch of flying, the transition upward to the more complex airplanes is quick and easy, because flying will have become a reflexive response, leaving your mind open to cope with things like retracting the landing gear, setting the propeller controls, and other diverse demands of a high-performance airplane.

There is also no real harm done if you have to switch brands of airplanes during your student days. Because there were no real flight schools and airplanes were scarce in my corner of East Texas years ago, I began with Ray Gannaway in the Aeronca *Champ* with the *stick* in my right hand and the throttle in my left. After six hours, the owner took his little airplane and left. I went over to Orange County airport and met A. G. Vanneman, who was teaching in a *Luscombe*. New instructor, stick in my left hand, throttle in my right. About six more hours of that and I soloed the Luscombe and Van got a brand-new Champ and I was back to flying the other way. About midway through student flying, somebody ran the new Champ out of gas, hit a levee, and knocked the wheels out from under it. It went into the hangar and I went back to Jefferson County and found Gannaway again, and he borrowed a Cub for us to fly in. Now we were seated in tandem (fore-and-aft) with me in the rear, trying to see the instrument panel through Ray in the front. Four hours in the wonderful little Cub, then the Champ was fixed over in Orange again, and I went back there. But just before it was time for my private pilot check ride flight somebody dinged the Champ again and a lady student hit a ditch landing the Luscombe, flipped it over on its back, undid her seat belt, fell on her head, got excited and opened the door and ran the entire length of the fabric-covered wing in her high heels.

Van, not yet discouraged, took me out to fly my check ride in a four-place *Cessna 172* which was brand-new and the first one we had seen around those parts. That bright aluminum thing looked as big as a DC-3 to me. I had never flown a nose-wheel tricycle-gear airplane before—all the others had been the *taildragger* type, old-fashioned airplanes that sat raked up in front with their tails resting on a little third wheel in the back. And I had never flown an airplane that had wing flaps. And here we were on that all-important flight test, with all this new stuff to learn, and my knees clanking that my mouth needed more water.

Vanneman leaned over in the seat, showed me how to operate all that stuff, and told me to calm down—"It's just another airplane."

Well, that made sense. So I flew it just like another airplane. Heavier on the controls, but easier to land. I passed my ride "thumbs up." And Van's words were prophetic.

Years later, on my first landing of a twin-engined *turboprop* aircraft, I got the fidgets. Ray "Big Deal" Goodwin beside me said, "Settle down, it's just another airplane." Same thing Earl West said the first time we walked out to the Stearman. Just looking up at that narrow-legged, naked, hairy-engined biplane with its propeller hub higher than my head scared me to death. "It's just another airplane," said the taciturn West, and it was. Just another wonderful, exciting, beautiful, mind-filling airplane.

So let us now take a look at the training planes, starting with the big three: Cessna, Piper and Beechcraft. We'll also talk about the little *Grumman American.* Then move on back into history to some of the older two-seaters that you might still encounter: the Champ, Cub, *Taylorcraft*, and *Ercoupe*.

Clearly dominating the field are the high-winged Cessnas and the low-winged Pipers, and there is the endless airport argument about which is best. "If the good Lord had wanted wings on the bottom, he'd have built birds that way," say the Cessna pilots. "All big serious airplanes are low-winged, so why not start in one?" says Piper. And the Beechcraft trainer looks so much like the earlier Piper that you might wonder at the possibility of incest among aircraft designers. The choice between the three is so inconsequential that I would learn to fly in whichever one came with the instructor and school I liked best.

Today's Cessna 152 is the logical outgrowth of a postwar design. It bears a strong family resemblance in both appearance and handling to its bigger brothers in the Cessna line. All-metal, with side-by-side seating, it has a lingering glide and tends to float out and prolong landings. The spring-steel landing gear is strong but bouncy.

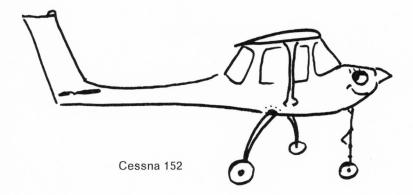

Cessna 152

The Piper Tomahawk and the Beech Skipper are both designs of the late 1970s. Both all-metal, also with side-by-side seating, these low-winged *monoplanes* are a step toward giving the pilot increased visibility. Both use the airline "mod stylishness" of mounting the *horizontal stabilizer* high atop the rudder. Both glide and land predictably, but with little floating.

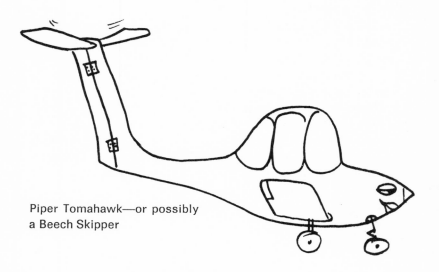

Piper Tomahawk—or possibly
a Beech Skipper

The Piper 140 is the trainer replaced by the Toma-hawk. An older design, but still very much in use at flight schools, it is the two-seater version of the basic Piper Cherokee series which successfully grew on up into larger and more sophisticated Pipers. The popular 140 is not known for prolonged glides or any floating around before it lands.

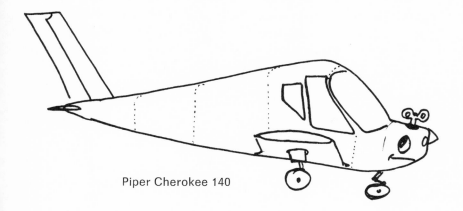

Piper Cherokee 140

The Grumman American, the smallest of the trainers, seats two side-by-side under a fighter-plane-style sliding canopy. Its stubby wings are of unusual bonded aluminum fabrication instead of being riveted, and it has a free-castering nose wheel. Glides steeply, doesn't float around at all on landing.

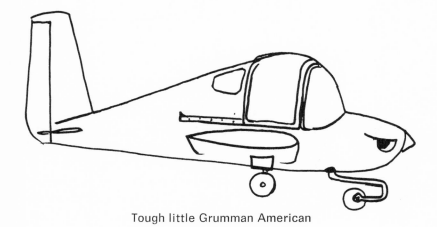

Tough little Grumman American

The legendary Cub was the first low-cost, low-powered small airplane. With Gilbert Taylor's design and Bill Piper's money, the Cub opened the skies to student flying in the early 1930s. The basic design of this gentle airplane is so good that Piper still builds it today as the big-engined Super Cub, now used more by *bush pilots* than by students. It's sensitive, and not as easy to fly as the new Piper Tomahawk, but a Cub will teach you more. Few are used for instruction today.

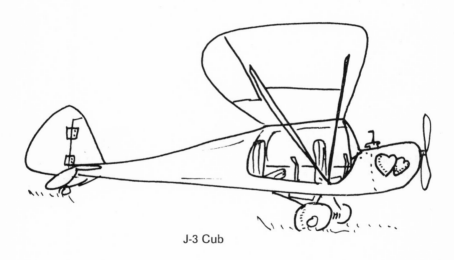

J-3 Cub

Mr. Piper and Mr. Taylor were not long to each other's liking. Shortly after the advent of the Cub, Mr. Taylor split and created a new design, the Taylorcraft. All-fabric-covered like the Cub, the T-Craft was fatter, seated its two passengers side-by-side, and gave them control wheels instead of a stick to fly by. Although faster, and just as responsive as a Cub, the T-Crafts were never built in large numbers. But like the Cub, this design was so good that in 1981 it is still being hand-built in the original factory by the original descendants, and the little airplanes are cherished. More demanding than the Cub to fly well, they float on forever instead of landing.

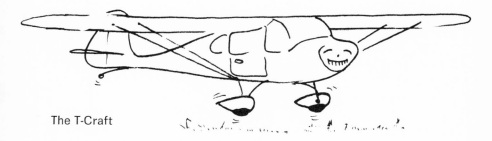

The T-Craft

This next aircraft was first known as the Aeronca (Aeronautical Corporation of America), then as the Champ, and in later beefed-up versions as the Citabria (which spells Airbatic backward). All-fabric-covered like the Cub, it also seats two in tandem with stick controls, only in the Champ the student gets to sit in front. Not as sensitive as the Cub, or as demanding of coordination as the T-Craft, the Champ, still in use at many small airports, is a light plane without fault.

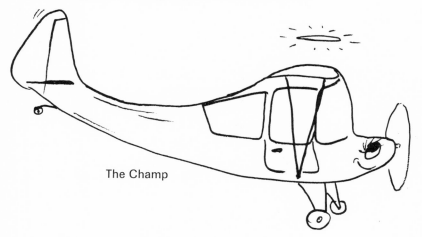

The Champ

Luscombes persist. Born out of larger, faster airplanes by Don Luscombe in the postwar flurry of new designs, the Luscombe was never much of a high-volume seller. Yet of the few that were made, nearly all must be roosting in hangars at rural airports. Luscombes persist. One reason, perhaps, is that they are so strong. With a metal ice-cream cone for a fuselage, topped by a thin, narrow, fabric-covered wing, the Luscombe seats two, knees to chin, side-by-side. It has stick controls and a transomlike windshield to peer dimly out of. The Luscombe is fast, aerobatic, and wicked to land. Fly a Luscombe too slow and it stalls. At once. Quits flying. Stall it deep enough and it spins. But it recovers from stalls and spins as quickly as it enters into them. And on the ground, with its narrow, high, stiff-legged landing gear, the Luscombe is good proof that an airplane will do what it looks like it will do. It's not really a beginner's training plane, but Van neglected to mention this to me, so I thrashed it in and out of the cornfields. We never hurt each other, and now I never shut up about having soloed in a Luscombe.

Luscombe

Fred Weick's Ercoupe, like the Chrysler Air-Flow sedan, was too good an idea, too far ahead of its time. Designed to be a stallproof, spinproof, easy-to-fly every-man's airplane, the Ercoupe suffered from that "other face" of flying. Ercoupe pilots were suspected of not having enough of the Right Stuff. Safe, and introducing new concepts in design, this little metal-bodied, fabric-winged two-seater placed its occupants side-by-side in a cleanly designed, high-visibility, raised-cockpit canopy that was very similar to the new Beech and Piper train-ers. It introduced tricycle landing gear when all the air-planes that outsold it had to be wrestled to a stop with the third wheel on the wrong end. Ercoupes were not only easy to land, but were so stable in flight that the early ones had no rudder controls: you just steered it like a car. Rudders and *ailerons* were interconnected through the control wheel. Retrofit rudder controls were later offered in an attempt to improve sales and make it more complicated to fly. It's not likely that you will learn to fly in an Ercoupe, but they should be mentioned so you'll know what it is when you see one—sun faded, near abandoned, sitting at the far end of the ramp, chin-deep in weeds.

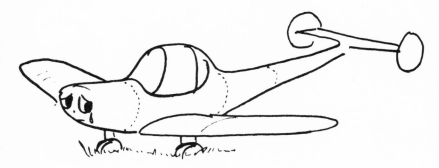

Ercoupe

These brief notes touch lightly on only the most commonly found airport two-seaters. Coming to recognize the array of past, present, domestic, foreign and homebuilt airplanes is part of the fun of hanging around the airport. Listening to the lies that pilots tell about them is part of the lore.

HOW SAFE
IS THIS THING?

Newspapers love a good, clean airplane-crash story. Let one of your locals be carried away on silvered wings and they move all the rape and robbery stories to inside pages. An airplane accident is front-page.

Let a local pilot deftly land his ailing aircraft on a farm road or field, and before he can walk away unscathed he has drawn a crowd of reporters. There he is, grinning on the front page, telling of his miraculous escape from the jaws of death. How embarrassing.

All this is most unfortunate, for it perpetuates the old legend that flying is a dangerous and derring-do affair. As a veteran reporter, I should point out to you some obvious logic. "News" is still the telling of the unusual. "Man Bites Dog" is what sells papers. Airplane wrecks are still "news." On a holiday weekend a dozen of your fellow humans might die in car wrecks and each will get only hometown regrets. But if one dies in a plane crash the story is still spectacular enough to go statewide. Aviation accidents are uncommon enough to still be "news," but their high visibility might worry your family and even yourself as you consider learning to fly.

Some of the questions uppermost but unspoken in the mind of a newcomer to aviation are: How stoutly is this thing built? What kind of mechanical condition is it in? How safe is flying?

Aviators love to tell you that the most hazardous part of the trip is behind you as soon as you get out of your car. Not so. But according to National Transportation Board statistics, boating is more dangerous than flying little airplanes. Still, buying a ticket and flying on a scheduled airliner is safer than flying one yourself. Staying home in bed is even safer than that.

Most general-aviation mishaps are traced to an error in judgment or poor flying technique. And this is most often such a simple thing as running out of gas, or flying into bad weather. So set yourself this early goal of planning to learn all the common-sense techniques and judgmental values that you can. I hope this does not discourage you, but a Navy study revealed that a person's driving record tends to reflect what kind of a pilot he is going to be.

On the question of the mechanical condition of the airplane, automobiles should have it so good. By federal law your training plane gets an annual inspection of every hinge, cable, fitting, engine part, and accessory it's got. The airplane is pretty well taken apart and brought up to factory specs for its annual. And all airplanes for hire—that is, for commercial use such as training—also get a one-hundred-hour inspection. This is similar to the annual, but involves only the most common and everyday inspection and preventive work. Also, any well-maintained airplane gets an oil change at twenty-five hours; the mechanic usually checks the spark plugs, too.

All these inspections and maintenance items, except for the most simple, are performed by an aviation mechanic whose license was harder for him to get than the one you are going for now. And there are two log books that stay in the airplane: *airframe* and engine. The mechanic logs a description of the work done in these permanent and official documents, and signs it off with his own precious name and certificate number. Wouldn't you love to see auto mechanics doing that?

The final and most critical inspection of the airplane is the one you will do before each flight. It was an early tradition, and long since a law, that the man who's going to fly the thing has the last say over whether or not it's *airworthy*. Also a part of the old tradition is that nobody snorts or scoffs at you if, after the pre-flight inspection, you refuse to fly the plane.

Good maintenance is a serious and everyday part of aviation.

Now, as to the first doubting question: How stoutly is this thing made? A factory-built airplane is the nearest thing you will ever find to something that technically came down an assembly line but is actually handcrafted. If one of the rivets that holds the aluminum skin of an airplane together is canted, dimpled in too deep, or improperly flared, it gets found, circled with a wax pencil, drilled out, and done over. The excessive amount of handwork and piecework that goes into an airplane is one of the reasons they cost so much.

Before an airplane goes into production the prototype must be flown through certification test flights by engineering test pilots. After an airplane is certified, each and every one is taken out and flown by a production test pilot to make sure this individual airplane does exactly what it is certified to do.

Every single part in the airplane—rivets, nuts, bolts, all of it—must be certified before it can be built into the plane. This certification process can take years. Done by the maker himself but to FAA standards, the tedious certification process is one of the reasons for the reluctance of the makers to change anything. That, and the characteristic conservatism of the aircraft manufacturing industry.

And these light, flimsy-looking, stamped-out airplanes are surprisingly strong. Part of the certification of a training plane is that its wings must be able to bear four times its normal weight. That means that an average 2,000-pound training plane has wings that will bear an 8,000-pound load. And that's just the test before anything bends. There is strength beyond that.

One happy result of all this care and caring is that, unlike automobiles, airplanes last forever. Barring damage, or corrosion, an old airplane that is well cared for just gets older and worth more money. Many of the wartime DC-3s are still in daily commercial service. My own 1968 Mooney Ranger is not unusual in its being worth now about twice what I paid for it. The one ray of sunshine in the clouds of rising costs of flying is that a good airplane is a good investment.

Unlike auto engines, which just run until they quit or until the body rots off from around them, aircraft engines have a manufacturer's recommended span of useful life. Engine life is measured in terms of hours of use, and the TBO (time before overhaul) of a good light-plane power plant is between 1,200 and 2,000 hours. Average use of a private plane is a surprisingly low 200 hours per year, although training planes in use every day roll up their hours much faster than that.

When an engine reaches TBO, the private owner groans and forks up the few thousand for an engine exchange or for having his present engine rebuilt to factory-new specs. The big flight schools usually replace their fleet at about half TBO. You can read the hours on the engine of any plane by looking at the total on the Hobbs meter, or on the tachometer.

Once, when I was flying the old Stearman biplane which belongs to George Mitchell of M&M Air Service (a large *ag flying* outfit in Beaumont, Texas), I went in and told his chief pilot, Earl West, that the old radial engine sure was running smooth. West grinned at me with the other face of flying and said, "When they get smooth like that they're fixing to swarm you."

Actually, airplane engines are quite simple and seldom experience catastrophic failure. Airplanes have limped back and landed with such awful-sounding things as blown cylinder heads, broken crankshafts, stuck valves, burned pistons. An airplane engine nearly always warns the pilot that something is going wrong by a partial power failure. It slows down and, as we say, begins *running rough.*

Within a few short hours you will get so accustomed to how a healthy airplane engine sounds that any change in its tone will activate long-unused ear muscles and cause your ears to get pointy and stand right up. One of the bits of other-face humor in flying is that when you're crossing hostile terrain such as forests, lakes, or rocks in a single-engine plane, the engine sooner or later goes into "auto rough," or "over-water rough." This is a pilot-induced symptom caused by an overactive imagination in a situation where there is no good landing place available.

In all my happy years of flying I have never had an engine just pack up on me and quit cold in a situation where I could not get the ailing airplane back down onto a runway. Of course, knowing where the nearest runway is at all times is a great help in bringing a getting-sick airplane back home again. Part of your training syllabus will be how to recognize and cope with in-flight emergencies and other "what if" situations.

The entire structure of student flying is oriented around safety. "To safely perform . . ." is the most often repeated qualification in the Federal Air Regulations under the subtitle "Aeronautical Skill." Statistically, the record of private flying improves slightly each year. But within those same statistics the broadest column is still the vague but meaningful "faulty pilot technique." This dark tent loosely covers most of the "he-just-shoulda-known-betters." Running into instrument weather, running out of gas, and running out of airspeed still add up to over half the accident causes. Much time is spent with the student in recognition and avoidance of these hazards, and nearly all of them violate at least one clearly written FAR.

Crashes, for the most part, are perfectly good-running airplanes being driven into the ground by someone who decided the rules didn't really apply to him. As you stand at the threshold of flying and wonder how safe it is, remember that the primary accident cause is squirming right there inside your own skull. Only you can control that.

THE
WALK-AROUND

This chapter will tell you the names and functions of the main parts of the airplane so that you can carry on a meaningful conversation with those folks out at the airport.

You could learn much of this same language by the double-sensory input of building a simple plastic scale-model airplane from a kit. Name the parts and touch them; the kit plans use real nomenclature.

I don't intend to go into all aeronautical engineering and background theory about the parts of an airplane. You could fly forever and not know why an airplane flies. If your intellectual curiosity draws you into this, there are many serious textbooks on every phase of the subject.

In the wood-and-fabric days when I fell in love with airplanes I just went out to the airport and there it was —the airplane. The plane was willing, Gannaway was willing, and I was eager, so we just got into it and flew away. Not any more unnatural than having an affair with a girl before you have read any of the sex manuals. That plane and I quickly learned what we needed to know about each other.

In the demonstration flight and the walk-around inspection of the airplane you can learn the names of the major parts and get a basic grasp of their function.

The airplane rests on its *landing gear*, which consists of a pair of main wheels and the steerable nose wheel. The brakes are in the hubs of the main wheels, and those structural members which connect the wheels to the fuselage, or the body of the plane, are called *struts*. In high-winged aircraft and in biplanes those bracing members from fuselage to wing, or between the wings, are also called struts.

The wing, which is the lifting surface when in flight, is measured tip to tip for its *span*, and *leading edge* to *trailing edge* for its *chord*. The curved upper surface of the wing has a *camber* giving it a long teardrop profile called the *airfoil*.

Those hinged control surfaces at the outboard trailing edge of the wing are the ailerons. In a neutral position they both trail, streamlined, as a part of the shape of the airfoil, but in their function of banking the airplane into a turn they move in opposite directions. They control the *roll axis* of the plane, which is one of the four free movements in flight that an airplane is capable of. An airplane can *thrust* forward, *pitch* up or down, or *yaw* its nose from side to side in addition to turning on the roll axis. Moving the control wheel to the left will raise the left aileron, lower the right one, deflect the wing out of level flight, and begin a bank and turn to the left. Opposite movement of the control wheel will roll it back level again.

Also hinged to the trailing edge of the wing, but inboard of the ailerons, are the *flaps*. Wing flaps move only downward, and they move together. Birds use flaps

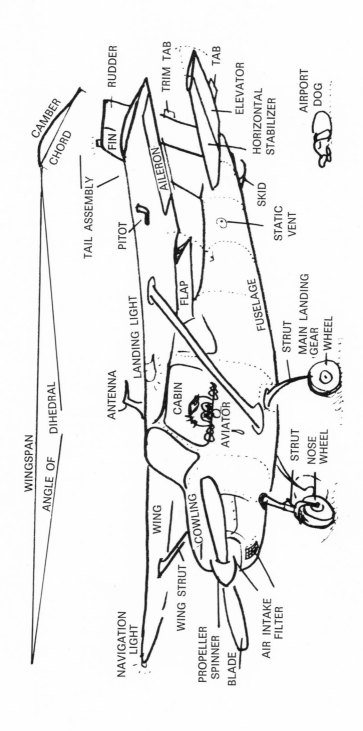

WINGSPAN

ANGLE OF DIHEDRAL

CAMBER

CHORD

TAIL ASSEMBLY

FIN

RUDDER

TRIM TAB

AILERON

TAB

ELEVATOR

HORIZONTAL STABILIZER

PITOT

SKID

STATIC VENT

AIRPORT DOG

LANDING LIGHT

FLAP

FUSELAGE

ANTENNA

CABIN

AVIATOR

STRUT

MAIN LANDING GEAR

WHEEL

STRUT

NOSE WHEEL

WING

COWLING

NAVIGATION LIGHT

WING STRUT

PROPELLER SPINNER

BLADE

AIR INTAKE FILTER

in landing: They spread out their trailing-edge feathers, sort of cup their airfoil to increase lift and drag in order to slow down and better regulate their rate of descent, and perch neatly upon the intended twig. Pilots use flaps for much the same reasons. In older airplanes flap controls were a direct-acting mechanical lever situated between the seats. Modern trainers use electrically powered flaps, the switch located low and center on the instrument panel within reach of both seats. In either system, flaps can be lowered in controlled increments from partial to full, and there is usually an indicator somewhere in the cockpit showing the degree of flaps in use.

The other primary control surfaces of an aircraft are on the *tail assembly*. The vertical portion of this is the *fin*, with the rudder hinged on behind it. The rudder controls the yaw axis of the plane: Right foot on the right rudder pedal will yaw the nose to the right; left foot, left rudder, does the opposite.

The small wing of the tail assembly is called either the *stabilizer* or the *horizontal fin*. The *elevators* are the movable surfaces hinged to the back of the stabilizer, and they control the pitch axis. Moving the control wheel back raises the elevators and pitches the nose of the plane upward, and vice versa.

Some modern trainers combine the elevator and stabilizer into one movable part which is then called the *stabilator*. But nobody uses that cobbled-up word much; the stabilator is often as not just called "the elevators" in common usage. Some of us think stabilator-equipped airplanes are a little more abrupt in pitch control than those with a conventional stabilizer and elevator.

For most of their history airplanes were as functional in their appearance as steam locomotives. Form followed function, and the results are now called "classics." A little bit of styling trendiness began to creep into light-aircraft design when vertical fins and rudders were swept back *à la* Boeing 707 jet transport. When big jets went to engines aft they had to move the horizontal tail plane up on top of the vertical fin to get it out of the way of jet blast. With this T-tail design as the sure mark of a modern airplane, light-plane makers began to introduce T-tails, too. At this writing the debate is still on as to whether a conventional piston-engined light plane flies better or worse with a jet-style T-tail.

There is one more control surface on the tail assembly which does not act as a primary mover of an axis, but serves to refine such movement. The elevator *trim tab* is a small hinged panel set into the trailing edge of the elevator. While the elevator may be in a neutral position, the small trim tab can be raised or lowered, causing a sort of fine-screw adjustment to the pitch level of flight. The trim-tab control is usually a saucer-sized wheel, set low and centered between the pilots. It is geared so that a discernible hand movement in rotating the wheel will cause only the most minute movement of the trim tab. In effect the trim tab gives a fine-tune adjustment to the airplane in flight, and helps to balance things so that the plane can be flown hands off for a while. If in level flight you notice that there is a lingering back pressure on the yoke against your hand, you can "trim it out" so that stick pressures are neutral again. More sophisticated aircraft have trim tabs on all three axes—elevators, rudders, and ailerons. I wish all planes did. On a long, level trip the airplane will fly itself for hours in a state of perfect balance and stability with just a little tweaking of the trim tabs.

Some pilots like to fly with the airplane slightly out of trim, feeling a little pressure from the yoke in the hand, but one of the pilots I admire most always flies with the airplane trimmed out to be stable and balanced at any power setting or attitude. Earl West is a corporate pilot now, flying heavy, fast twins, but for the first thirty-one years he was a crop duster, an ag pilot, one of the most dangerous of aviation jobs. Earl flew the same old converted Stearman biplane, flew it as much as 1,000 hours a year. He probably has more Stearman time than any man alive. He flew it at gross weight on hot days, flew it low and slow in steep turns. Earl taught me to fly Stearmans, and I watched every little thing he did. Whatever his secrets are, they are worth copying. And Earl West always flew the Stearman in neutral trim, "except when my wheels were brushing the crop tops. Then I flew a little up-trim so it would climb in a moment of inattention."

It didn't seem to me that the trim needed to be fussed with that much. The Stearman has very light stick forces through the elevators. It rolls like a truck, but pitches up or down with fingertip pressures. (So does the old Mooney I bought many years later, and I was at home with it. Thanks again, Earl.) Earl is not a talkative man; he never discussed trim with me, then or now, but sitting in the rear cockpit while he flew it from the front, I watched his every little movement reflected in my own set of controls. On the Stearman the trim control is a little lever, mounted on the left behind the throttle. Every time Earl West made any power change that upset the pitch forces of that old biplane, that trim lever moved a tiny bit. Every time he climbed or began a descent I could see that he was stroking that trim lever, bringing the airplane back into neutral stick forces. At the time I couldn't see why. Unlike bigger, faster airplanes yet to come where a landing or takeoff attempt with the elevator out of trim would set up stick forces stronger than a man could handle, the Stearman was always light and quick in the elevators.

Earl was teaching me basic good habits. I pass them along to you from the sun-weathered ole master in helmet and goggles: Use the trim tab. Fly with the airplane in balance.

The propeller is on the nose of the airplane. The British, being an older and more civilized people, call the propeller an "air screw." That more aptly describes what it does. You can look at its inclined blades and visualize how the engine-driven whirling prop creates the *thrust* to give an airplane its forward movement.

Most of the racket from an airplane in flight comes from the propeller, the tips of which may be moving at the speed of sound and be doing their own sonic booming. It is because of the high velocity of the air moving over the prop tips that the casual-looking pre-flight gesture of running one's fingertips along the edges of the propeller blade is so important. That is not a loving caress, although it well could be. The stroke is to feel for nicks, deep scratches, or upset metal along the edges where the prop blade may have struck loose gravel while taxiing.

There is always some gravel at the airport, and even if you reduce power and coast through it, the prop sucks it into the blades like a vacuum cleaner. The result is that after a time a propeller comes to look like a battered old broadsword. Don't fly a prop with a crack you can see, nor one with a nick or a dent that would cup a pencil diameter. At high tip speeds such minor damage will set up stresses that might cause a prop-tip separation— which would leave the propeller so unbalanced that it would create a vibration severe enough to shake the engine out of its mounting. Dressing down, or smoothing out the angles of such dings, with a fine-cut file, is one of the things a pilot can do by way of maintenance —although it's always better to leave this to a mechanic.

The other danger of the propeller is that when it's whirling you can't see it, and in the background noise of the airport, may not even hear it. Therefore I have set myself some hard and fast propeller rules:

- Don't ever offer any part of your body to the propeller arc, even if the airplane has been sitting still so long that weeds have grown around its tires. Just never do it. That way you never will.
- Watch how many airport people duck in and out of the blades of a parked airplane with a still-hot engine, one that might just kick over half a snort all on its own. When you touch the blades in pre-flight, reach way out and touch them so that if the prop moved it would move away from you. Sometimes there is no cure for having to reach inside the cowling front to check the V-belt, but intrude into the propeller arc as little as possible, and never casually.
- Never let passengers disembark while the engine is running. This is usually a joyful time—lots of noise, excitement, blasts of wind. There is no way you can stop the

Propeller arc—place not to stand in

engine in time, nor shout a warning, if your friend starts to walk into the propeller.

• If you are shoving the airplane back into a parking slot on the ground, push only against the hub or center of the prop. This is not only a safety measure; pushing hard against a prop blade tip could deflect it out of alignment.

Despite all of these warnings, propellers are hardy and not a troublesome part of airplanes. But do give them all the respect you would a lethal weapon. They can be.

A part of your outside walk-around inspection before flight will involve checking the oil, the gas, and the fuel drain system. No matter how much trouble it is, always remove the gas-tank caps and see to it that the tank is full. Airplane gas gauges are just not that good.

Another part of the outside ritual is called "draining the sumps." Moisture condenses in partly filled fuel tanks, accumulating a little water in the bottom, and although no two do it alike, all the makers provide a means of draining small samples from the lowest part of the fuel system and tanks. There should be a little clear plastic cup in the airplane that has a prong at the top which will fit into these under-the-tank drains and allow you to catch and see a sample from the tank bottom. This is one of the few old-time grubby pilot deeds left for you to do with a clean modern airplane. On low-winged planes you get to reach up under there; all of them dribble some good-smelling av-gas on your hand. A wetting ritual before the mystic flight.

What you are looking for is water in the gas tank. The water settles to the bottom, drains out first. In the clear plastic cup you can see any water, separate from the gas. Keep filling the cup and tossing the sample aside until you drain down only pure gasoline. (Not a good

Draining the sumps—one of the last of the old-time rituals

time to be cupping a cigarette.) On the last sample when you see no more water, gaze into the cup to make sure that the gasoline is the color it's supposed to be. Different airplanes run on different kinds of fuel, and the refineries dye the fuel different colors for identification. Airports may pump several different kinds of fuel from adjoining pumps, and nobody will be as interested in seeing to it that you have the right fuel as you should be. The 80-octane is red, 100-octane low-lead is blue.

Next, open the little access door in the cowling and look at the oil dipstick. At least once a year some dilbert will forget this and take off with no oil in the engine. The only advantage to this is that the engine only lasts until right after takeoff, thus making the wreck easier to find.

Last of the items on the outside are the *pitot* tube and the *static system vent*. The pitot tube is the little L-shaped pipe just below one wing and sticking out forward of the leading edge. A simple device, it is mounted outside the propeller arc in undisturbed air, and as the airplane gains forward speed and altitude the varying amount of air pressure that travels through its little plumbing system to the instrument panel is what activates the mechanism of the airspeed indicator. The small opening of the pitot tube is a favorite lodging for dirt daubers, spiders, other small insects, and sometimes bits of blown twigs or grass. Peek into the pitot; any obstructions will be in front, ahead of the metal rain baffle. A toothpick is an ideal digging-out tool. And for goodness sakes don't ever blow into the pitot tube to clear it. You will wreck an expensive, fine instrument with that hurricane of breath. The pitot static system is a source of pressure for operations of the airspeed indicator, the *altimeter*, and the *vertical speed indicator*.

The static system vents are located flush with the fuselage skin—dime-sized, bright-metal fittings near the tail. Some planes have one on each side. Look here to see that the static vents are open. The most common problem is finding them closed with paste wax by some well-meaning soul who was only beautifying the airplane.

In the owner's manual the walk-around inspection is depicted as a routine sequence of events, best performed in the same pattern each time. Do it that way. Before you leave the propeller at the nose section, look to see that the nose-wheel tire is not low or bald, and while you're under there, just glance around to be sure nothing is leaking. From the pitot tube as you go around the wing tip, give the aileron a brotherly shake, look at its hinges, see if all the nuts, bolts, and fasteners are still with you. Same thing with the tail group, I have never found anything missing or loose doing this, but I still always give everything a look and a shake while doing the outside walk-around. This is really the very best time to discover whether there is something wrong with the flying machine.

Once you know everything is in order, it's time to get into the cockpit.

IN THE COCKPIT

Had you been an old barnstormer flying biplanes, you would now crawl into the cockpit. In today's light aircraft it's the cabin, but we still sometimes call it the cockpit. On large aircraft the partitioned forward part of the cabin where the pilots sit is called the flight deck, except some of *them* still say cockpit, too.

"Cockpit" is just a good old romantic term. Perhaps it began when Montgolfier's balloon ascended before the King of France and a crowd of 30,000 on September 19, 1783. This first flight carried aloft a sheep, a duck, and a cock. Thus cockpit? (But why not "duckpit"?) *Webster's* lists the aeronautical use of space for seating the pilot and passengers as a third choice, the first for cockpit being "a pit for cockfights, hence a region of many conflicts." Second, "the pit of a theater."

Your future experiences in this region of conflict may support *Webster's* first choice for "cockpit." Your initial glance at the dial-and-switch-studded instrument panel with all its levers and knobs may be a little intimidating.

One of my favorite cartoons is a view of an airliner flight deck with the old captain saying to the co-pilot, "No kidding, there was once a time when I knew what they're all for."

In real life the pilot damn well knows what they are all for and can operate the controls in the dark with his eyes shut. It's not as difficult as it looks. The controls needed to fly an airliner are basically the same as you will find in the cockpit of the trainer, only there are more of them to go along with the multiple engines and the backup redundancy of all the flight instruments and navigation and communication equipment.

In all probability you could not, right now, sit down and draw a sketch of the instrument panel and controls of the car you drive every day. Yet you don't have to stop and grope or consciously think about such things when you are threading five-o'clock traffic. Your eye, hand, and foot fly to the right spot from habit. That is how it should be, and soon will be, with you and the little airplane. No one will think you are funky if during your flying career you sit alone in the cockpit of a parked airplane that you intend to fly and practice naming and touching things until you can do it with your eyes shut.

Although no two cockpits are alike, not even in airplanes of the same make and model, there is a certain logical sequence and placement of all the instruments and controls. Most obvious are the dual-control wheels. Then the matching brake and rudder pedals up under the instrument panels where your feet rest upon them naturally. The knobs or levers sticking out from the lower center of the instrument panel are the engine controls. Near them in the lower center are the flap and trim controls. *Flight instruments*, those having to do with the direction and *attitude* of the airplane in flight, are grouped in front of the left seat. The radios that you will both navigate and communicate with are centered in the instrument panel, called the *radio stack* or *radio deck*. The engine instruments are usually in front of the right seat.

That's the basic configuration, and the detailing that follows is in no way intended to describe any one airplane. Designers are approaching standardization, but it's been a long time coming. Hard-to-find controls, and similar-looking knobs that serve vastly different functions, have long plagued pilots and have resulted in confusion, delays, and tragicomic mixups. There is hoary old hangar humor about the easily confused landing-gear retraction and flap retraction switches on high-performance aircraft. Question: How can a Texas Aggie tell if he has landed and retracted the wheels instead of the flaps? Answer: It takes full power to taxi to the ramp.

Let us approach our description of the cockpit details in the same sequence that these matters would come to your attention on a start-up, taxi out, flight, and landing.

First, position your seat to where you have a good view over the nose and everything is within easy reach. This I learned from Tex Maxwell, an Eastern Airlines pilot with whom I rode the flight deck many years ago when a civilian could still be invited to do that. He made a great production of adjusting the seat, muttering, "No matter what happens from here on, at least I will be sitting where I ought to be sitting." Aircraft have different degrees of seat adjustment, and some have a long travel on the floor tracks for fore-and-aft movement. When you have the seat where you want it, give a good shove off the rudder pedals to make sure it's really latched in place. There's nothing sillier-looking than a pilot who has applied takeoff power only to find that the thrust has unexpectedly propelled his seat back to where he can't reach anything. It happens now and then; makes for a wild takeoff.

Next, secure and snug down the seat belt. If you have shoulder harnesses, wear them. In airliners, automobiles, or private planes, seat and shoulder belts are just too good and simple an idea to neglect. Make it a habit and you'll feel naked without them.

The key goes into the ignition lock much as in a car. Next turn on the *master switch*. This opens electrical power from the battery to all the electrically driven devices on the plane except the engine. Don't flip the master on until you have made a check to see that all other individual switches for lights and radios are off. This is a practice that prolongs the life of lights and radios and batteries. This sequence is only a rough guide. Owner's manuals of individual makes and models, even the techniques of different instructors, will reveal many variations and exceptions to what we say here.

Before start-up make sure that the *fuel selector* is on. All aircraft have an on-off handle in the cockpit that cuts off the fuel flow from the tanks to the engine. And that's the only thing that fuel systems on different airplanes have in common. From there you will find different positions on different fuel selector switches to select from right tank, left tank, or both.

Learn the fuel management and layout of the fuel selection system of your airplane from the owner's manual and remember it more faithfully than you would your spouse's birthday or anniversary—the results of forgetting will be much worse. Something as dumb and simple as running out of gas is still a major cause of what we stiffly call "unscheduled landings."

Light planes carry a four- or five-hour supply of fuel onboard, which will outlast the average human bladder unless you are kin to a camel. But with the fuel selector on right tank or left, that awesome silence of running out of gas will come in about two hours if you forget to switch tanks. An airplane engine that quits from fuel exhaustion can be restarted easily enough if you are up high enough to spare the moments and altitude for that frantic four-handed game of switching to the full tank. A part of the certification of the airplane is that it can be restarted in flight. Your instructor will show you the procedure. But "if you are up high enough" is the key phrase to this business. And for that reason we consider it good flying to switch to the fuller tank after a long flight as your destination airport comes in sight.

Don't monkey with the fuel selector just before take-off. Have that all settled and done before you taxi out, so the time the engine will be running on the ground will be long enough to assure you that you are getting a good fuel flow from the selected tank.

Nearly all modern trainers carry their fuel in left- and right-wing tank cells. High-winged airplanes have the advantage of a simpler system—gravity feed. The fuel can just fall out of the wings down to the engine through the fuel lines. Low-winged airplanes have an engine-driven fuel pump to deliver the fuel, and this essential piece of hardware is backed up by a separate, electrically driven fuel pump called the *booster pump.* Some high-winged airplanes have a booster pump, too.

The booster is one of the electrical switches on the panel that you turn on before start-up to ensure a steady supply of fuel to the engine, and you leave it on during takeoff and prior to landing. Takeoff and landing with booster on is just the safety factor of having two fuel pumps working for you when you might need them the most. The two pumps run well with each other, but sooner or later all of us forget to turn off the booster and set sail for a long flight with it running. They are not made for continuous operation, and I can look in my fairly recent records and tell you exactly how much a replacement costs. They are expensive.

The last procedure for getting fuel to the engine before start-up is to *prime* it. Primer pumps vary from airplane to airplane, and you'll be instructed on how to use them. But on any night when the lights are still bright in the back of the hangar you will find gray-headed aviators gathered, each with his own idea of how much fuel prime is needed for hot engine, cold engine, winter or summer, high altitudes or low. For airplane engines as for women, no exact manual can ever be written on how much pre-start priming is too much or too little. Good luck.

With fuel on, booster on, engine primed, master on, you are now ready to bring the engine to life. In the olden days we used to crack the throttle, set the brakes, yell, "Contact!" and someone would spin the prop for us by hand. "Contact" meant the switch was on. Today we have what the Cajun French pilots along the Gulf Coast call "self-commencers"—self-starters, just like those on cars. And what we yell out of whatever window we can get open is "Clear!" This means to stand clear, that the propeller is about to begin turning. I don't know why we do that. You can see the nose, and determine if someone is standing too close. I guess it's a precaution for someone who may be crouched down out there, or for airport dogs who speak English. Anyway, we lean out and yell, "Clear!" It sounds good.

The airplane will want to start moving forward as soon as the engine is running, so set the brakes firmly now. To "crack" the throttle means to open it slightly. On most planes it's a matter of turning the ignition key to the "start" position and the airplane engine coughs to life. Prolonged cranking is bad form—drains the battery, heats up the starter. Five seconds is about enough cranking with no response. Stop, let things cool, go over your check list again.

The throttle is the dominant knob or lever in the engine controls cluster. It regulates how much fuel goes to the engine. Forward is more, back is less—this is now true for all engine controls. When the engine controls are push-pull knobs and when we raunchy old aviators are giving her all she's got—full power—we say, "Balls to the wall."

The smaller engine control next to the throttle is the *mixture control.* This is essential for aircraft because of the wide range of altitudes that an airplane engine runs in. The higher it goes, the thinner the air and the less oxygen available to support fuel combustion in the engine. If there were no mixture control an airplane engine running at 5,000 feet in the thin air would be getting more gasoline than it needs for a good combustion mixture. This would be called running too *rich.* The engine would run, but not as smoothly as it could, and would be wasting gas. So the mixture control is pulled back to *lean* out the fuel-air ratio to what the engine wants. You can hear it smooth out and develop a little more power. If you come back too far on the mixture control the engine gets rough again, and if you come back all the way it shuts off the fuel and the engine starves out and quits. For this reason the mixture control knob is usually red. Adjust it with care and caution.

For start-up on the ground the mixture is usually left at full rich—all the way forward—and the throttle is eased forward about an inch of its travel. Crank the engine to life, adjust the throttle so that the engine idles smoothly, and immediately look at the *oil pressure gauge.* If the oil pressure gauge has not come to life and is not indicating oil pressure, shut the engine down right now.

The engine of your trainer is a simple and rugged little piece of machinery, the design of which has remained fundamentally unchanged for over fifty years. Its four cylinders, lying flat, two on each side, are air-cooled. Without oil pressure to send lubricants to its hot little innards you may as well shut it down at once and avoid further damage, for it will heat up, seize, and shut itself down, ruined, in a minute or so anyway.

The oil pressure gauge is located over on the right in the engine instrument cluster, and near it you will usually see the *oil temperature gauge* and sometimes the *cylinder head temperature gauge.* It's customary to mark these instrument faces with a color-segmented arc: The broad green section is the normal operating range, with a warning redline at the high end. A wise pilot creates a habit of scanning his engine instruments regularly to be sure everything is still "in the green." If it's not, start looking for a place to land while you still have a choice, because there's a landing in your very near future.

This is not intended to create a sense of continuing apprehension within you, for as we said before, the little engines are sturdy and reliable. But as in humans, if something is about to go wrong inside, a change in temperature or pressure is often one of the early indications.

The temperature gauges are simple in design, and, unlike the fuel gauges, you can believe what they tell you. The oil pressure is activated as soon as the engine starts running. But as in a car, the temperature gauges take a little time to warm up, depending on the outside weather. Don't apply full power for takeoff until the oil has at least begun to show signs of warming up; on the other hand, be aware that in extremely hot weather prolonged ground operation can overheat the engine. Remember, the engine is air-cooled and tightly cowled. The propeller fans it some, turning it into the wind helps a little, but if your engine gets redline-hot on the ground, shut it down and let it cool.

The two-way radios and the radio beacon navigational systems in an airplane are called *avionics*. Your radio will be a duplex unit: One side is *nav* for navigation, the other side is *com* for communication. To avoid current surges to their delicate circuits, avionics should be switched on or off only when the engine is running.

At about $1,000 per pound, avionics are the most expensive and characteristically unreliable equipment on the airplane. Luckily, a dead radio in no way affects an airplane's ability to fly. The only problem might be that ground controllers will not know where you are, and if you rely solely on radio navigation, then sometimes *you* won't know either. That is one of the reasons you will be taught the old system of navigation by *dead reckoning*, using only the magnetic compass and clock.

At this time nobody seems to be sure why solid-state avionics are so faint-hearted. The manufacturers are men of goodwill and reputation. Flight schools do not skimp on buying the best and latest models of avionics. But all airliners and most general aviation aircraft carry more than one complete avionics system.

Because of the infamous temperamental nature of avionics, the FAA requires an accuracy check of some of the equipment within every thirty days of use. Compare that to the rest of the components of an airplane in private use which get by with an annual inspection, or one in commercial use which needs inspection only at hundred-hour intervals.

We will describe the operation of all these avionics once we get aloft.

10

OPEN THE CHUTE
AND LET 'EM OUT,
BOY!

That's what the announcer says at the rodeos in Texas when the bronc rider raises his hand and signals that he is ready for his ride: "Open the chute and let 'em out, boy!" What follows next is the roar of the crowd, wild riding, circling, bucking, pitching, the dust and thunder of hooves and high, thin, cowboy yells from the rider trying to stay in the seat.

This is what we hope to avoid in aviation.

Check list still in hand, you should be calmly and deliberately preparing your mount for takeoff. Don't hurry. Face into the wind if possible to get extra cooling for the engine, set the brakes, and begin the engine run-up.

You run up the engine by gently opening the throttle to the revolutions per minute (RPM) that your instructor asks for. Always move the throttle gently, whether opening or closing it. Only in lurid aviation writing does the pilot slam his throttle open. In real life, airplane engines tend to choke up and die when you do that.

The RPM are read off the *tachometer*, a dial among the engine instrument group which reads and works almost exactly like the "tach" in a sports car. Aircraft tachometer faces are color-coded into segmented arcs, much like the pressure and temperature gauges: redlined at the top, with a long green arc for safe operating range.

With brakes set and the engine now roaring at the higher power setting, we begin the simple but vital *mag check*.

Airplane engines develop their own electricity for the ignition spark that fires the spark plugs by a *magneto* system. It works independently of both the battery and the alternator, and is more reliable as a result. Once the engine is running the magnetos begin to generate their own electricity. Airplanes not only have this independent source of power to the spark plugs, they also have dual ignition systems. There are two magnetos and two sets of plugs and the engine is capable of running off of either half of the system.

This is a stellar safety feature, but an aircraft engine will not run with the ignition switch turned off.

Carl Neukirch, of the Skyhawks Sky Divers, based at Beaumont Municipal, tells of the hairy initiation ceremony they once gave the new pilot of the jump plane. At 12,000 feet, with the door of the Cessna 182 removed and all those animals in their jump suits and hard hats flying out into space, the last man pounded the pilot on the shoulder, gestured wildly at the instrument gauge cluster, gibbering in the roar of air. As the pilot leaned right to better peer at the engine instruments, the parachutist leaned over his left shoulder and turned off the engine, snatched the keys out, paused with a maniacal gleam in his eyes just before he tumbled backward out the door, dangling the bright keys before the pilot and shouting, "So long, turkey!"

The Skyhawks figure that any pilot who can't make a *dead stick* landing from 12,000 feet right over the field ought not to be flying the jump plane anyhow. The other face of aviation.

The next part of the run-up is to check the output and performance of each half of the ignition system. The ignition lock on little airplanes is marked off into four positions: "Off," "Right," "Left," and "Both." By switching the key to "Right" you are running the engine off the right magneto system only, and should be looking at the face of the tach when you do this. There will be a drop in RPM because any twin-ignition engine runs better with both sets of plugs firing. But if there is a marked drop, say 150 to 200 RPM, then you have a sick mag or fouled plugs or both and the flight will be a "downer." Don't go. Same thing for the "Left" side. Come back to the "Both" position each time to let the engine regain full power between tests.

There is no rule about the order of a mag check, so do it the way your instructor does. I always go to the position farthest away from "Both," then back to "Both," then to the one nearest to "Both." This is just my own habit pattern to be certain that I don't take my hand off the switch until it's back on "Both" again. An airplane will take off and fly on a single mag, but doing so is a dumb oversight by a preoccupied pilot and negates the built-in safety of the dual system.

If it's possible I prefer to take off with `both` fuel tanks on, *both* fuel pumps on, and *both* magnetos on. And if I had two sets of brains I'd want them *both* on.

I usually check the carburetor heat next, since it's another tach readout routine relating to the engine group. The carburetor heat control knob is often one of those in the row of knobs along the bottom edge of the panel. It sometimes looks and feels just like the cabin heater knob, cabin fresh-air knob, cigarette lighter, sometimes even the vital mixture control knob. So even after you get to know an airplane pretty well by touch, look and be sure you are operating the control you think you are operating. All we are doing when we pull out the carb heat knob briefly is to verify that this mechanical system is working.

The function of a carburetor heater is to prevent the formation of ice within the carburetor. This is a frequent but easily preventable cause for engine failure. What causes the ice to choke the throat of a carburetor is a combination of the vaporization and the expansion of the fuel mixture as it passes through the throat of the carburetor. The temperature of the mixture can drop as much as 60 degrees F. within a fraction of a second, and sometimes water vapor being "squeezed" out by this cooling will begin to form ice in the carb throat.

I am referring here to the temperature inside the carb, not in the outside air. Actually a carburetor is prone to start icing up on any high-humidity day when the outside temperature ranges from 20 to 70 degrees F. Oddly enough, there is almost no chance of a carburetor freezing on a dry, freezing day—no moisture in the air.

Carburetors are also likely to ice up when you reduce power, which is why you will learn as a habit to apply carburetor heat before coming back on the throttle to glide or land.

Carburetor ice is one of the things for you to worry about. The first sign that it's developing is a gradual loss of power, a roughness in the engine. When that happens, apply full carb heat, not partial. Come all the way back on the knob. The engine may run rougher at first as the ice melts and it digests all that water, but it soon smooths out to full power. Carb ice forms fairly often; it's easy to cure. The operation of the heater is simple, too: The knob just opens up a little bypass which allows heat from the exhaust system to enter into the little tin overcoat that the carburetor wears.

Heating the fuel mixture in the carburetor robs the engine of a little power, and that's the RPM drop you will see on the tach. This lets you know that the carb's overcoat is warm. Sooner or later, during landing practice to come, you will start a full-power takeoff with the carb heater still on. No real harm done except that it's robbing you of a little power and clearly indicating to your instructor what a bonehead you are. The carb heat knob is one engine control that you can slap shut.

Wouldn't you love to know the history of how early aviators found out about carburetor ice? The engine would roughen up and mysteriously quit, and by the time onlookers and investigators got to the crash all the ice was melted out and gone. Folks would walk off shaking their heads and saying, "If the Lord had meant for men to fly He would have given us wings."

Of course that's exactly what He did. He opened up our minds and we invented airplanes. But when I fly and use these age-old safety systems I always wonder how much it cost somebody way back then to figure out what was happening. Probably some early pilot was riding the wing with his own engine and when it started dying he poked his finger down in the carburetor just to find out what the hell was going on in there and found ice. Thanks, fella.

With the slight drop of RPM when you open and close the carb heat you know that device is working and you can now reduce the engine power to idle speed and lessen some of the clamor in the cockpit and get on with methodically going down your pre-flight check list.

Check the compass—the oldest instrument design on the airplane. As in the ancient seafaring style, the mag-

The probable discovery of carburetor ice

netic compass is gimbaled to float freely in alcohol, one part of it polarized to point always toward the earth's magnetic north. We also call it the *wet compass*. Show-offs and aviation writers sometimes call it the *whiskey compass* because its housing is full of alcohol.

The magnetic compass stands isolated, high above the center of the instrument panel. It is the only instrument on the airplane, except for the thermometer, that is not connected to some other system to make it work. When all else fails, you can still believe your magnetic compass.

The only trouble is that sometimes you can't read it. It will slosh and bounce around in rough air; its needle lags wistfully behind when you turn east or west away from the north pole, and rushes eagerly ahead of you when you are headed south and turn east or west toward the north pole. It will swing dizzily backward in a turn, even shift when you accelerate or slow down.

Magnetic compass needle always hating to leave north pole

The only time you can read a magnetic compass very well is during straight and level flight in smooth air. But even then it has two built-in errors. One is called *variation*. This term applies to the variation between the locations of the magnetic north pole that the compass points to, and the geographic north pole as depicted on maps.

The magnetic north pole is just about due north of the Great Lakes region, so in the United States the variation is about zero there, but increases the farther you go toward either coast. Part of your course will be a study of why we call it easterly variation out West, and westerly variation in the East. Some aeronautical charts depict the zero variation line as the *agonic line*, and show the increasing degrees of variation on across the country as *isogonic lines*. Today navigational headings from controllers are given in terms of magnetic headings, runways are numbered to magnetic north, and on radio navigational charts you will notice that the compass roses of the VOR stations are canted toward magnetic north, not the geographic north.

Here is my memory trick for remembering variation: It is kind of like politics in America—it leans a little to the right out West, and a little left in the East.

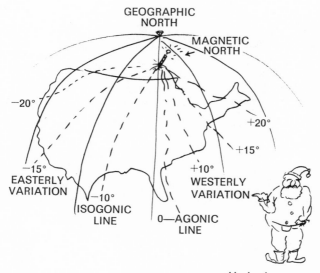

Ho ho ho—
You sure would think somebody
would have figured out a better
way of doing this.

When flying by radio navigational beacons, the variation is not a factor, but in dead-reckoning navigation—using the compass only—you need to understand variation.

Deviation is the other error within your magnetic compass. This is caused by the influence of the metal and electrical devices built into the airplane all around the compass. Upon installation, the compass is compensated for deviation as much as possible, but on some headings there will still be an error. The amount and direction of error is printed on a deviation card mounted to the compass of each airplane.

Magnetic compass being influenced by deviation (devil comes with airplane), and Variation (Vearth, daughter of Mother Earth)

I remember the word "deviation" as different from "variation" by thinking of the devious devils I carry with me onboard. An extreme example of temporary compass deviation was when Ed McKay was teaching me night flying. I brought a flashlight, as he said always to do on any night flight, but I brought a big one with one of those magnetic bases that you can stick to a metal wall. I set the flashlight right up on top of the instrument panel so I could find it easy—set it, in fact, right beside the magnetic compass. I was lost the whole night long, but I could always find my flashlight: The compass was pointing steadily right at it.

The simple little magnetic compass acts as a master compass to the *directional gyro* (DG) or, as it is also called, the *heading indicator*. This large flight instrument mounted directly in front of the pilot is not a compass at all but is used for direction finding more than the compass itself. The DG is built around a horizontally spinning, vacuum-powered *gyro*. It remains steady, is easy to read, and will accurately swing around counting off the actual degrees in your turn so well that precise 5-degree heading changes are common when flying by the DG, even in rough air.

But the DG, or heading indicator, does have a fault of its own: *precession*. This is gradual and predictable error which will creep in to such an extent that the DG must be reset to the magnetic compass about every fifteen minutes. The small error will vary depending on the mechanical condition of your individual DG. Resetting it is only a matter of pressing and twisting the knob until the DG reads the same as the magnetic compass. You will finally, after some embarrassing times of forgetting it, develop a nervous habit of resetting the DG. Only do it when the magnetic compass is steady in level cruise flight, and of course as a part of the pre-flight.

The random readings you see on the DG at pre-flight settings will remind you that for all its virtues, the DG has no idea of which way is north, only what you set into it from the old magnetic compass.

Couple of Sperry gyros remaining upright no matter what the airplane is doing

Gyro-driven flight instruments are essential to the all-weather utility of today's modern aircraft. The gyro offers considerable resistance to any forces that would move it from its own spin axis. It remains upright, no matter what the airplane is doing, and provides a level reference when the pilot can't find one. The first successful gyroscopic flight instrument, which was essential in the pioneering of instrument flying and remains basically unchanged fifty years later, is the *turn-and-bank indicator*. Here the gyroscope is coupled to a vertical indicator needle. When the airplane is banked into a turn the needle remains upright. A printed scale on each side of the needle indicates how far over the plane is banked and thus how steeply it is turning. The needle is broad, and has a predictable, easy-to-read movement about it—so much so that pilots have come to refer to a "one-needle-width turn" as a recognizable standard rate of turn.

There is an added feature on the turn-and-bank indicator that helps you determine whether the airplane is in a coordinated turn. It is situated beneath the needle, and looks like a small carpenter's level upturned in a slight smile. The liquid-filled glass tube contains a free-floating black ball about half an inch in diameter. When the airplane is banked and turned with no sideways slewing motion the ball stays centered. The turn-and-bank indicator is often as not called the *needle and ball*.

One other gyro-driven instrument complements the heading indicator and the turn-and-bank indicator in presenting the pilot with instrumented visualization of the attitude of his plane in flight. This is the *artificial horizon*, or *attitude indicator*. Once again a vacuum-driven gyro is used to create a steady reference point inside the moving aircraft. The artificial horizon display is very realistic. There is a horizon line across the middle of the face of this flight instrument and your little airplane appears to float freely in the sky. When you bank and climb the real airplane, the end-on view of the model banks its wings against the horizon and rises above the horizon, duplicating the movements of your flight path. Thus, the artificial horizon indicator gives a very graphic visualization of what your airplane is doing in flight. The instrument is reliable and needs no tending except to press and turn the knob during pre-flight to align the model's wings over the artificial horizon line.

Boy, you could have fooled me.

Artificial horizon indicator shows a climbing left turn.

Because these flight instruments are vacuum-driven, light aircraft have at least some means of warning you if the vacuum system is not working. Sometimes it is a warning light on the panel; but better is a gauge, often marked "suction," that gives you more than just a go or no-go readout.

An airplane can be flown without its vacuum pump working, but the vacuum-powered, gyro-driven flight instruments will obviously be inoperative. Sometimes the needle and ball instrument is marked DC and powered by an alternate source of electricity so that you don't lose all the gyros if the vacuum system fails. There is, unfortunately, no standard pattern among the manufacturers as to which gyros are spun by vacuum and which by electricity. This is some of the mystery you will have to learn about each individual airplane you fly.

Flying with a simulated failure of either the vacuum system or the electrical system will be a part of your regular training course. Usually the instructor will cover up some of the flight instruments and ask you to learn to fly "partial panel." It's not hard to do, and don't think that it will never happen to you. The service life of both vacuum pumps and alternators generating electricity is, according to a survey made recently by *Aviation Consumer* magazine, only about 700 hours of flight time. This does not compare favorably to the expected 2,000-hour life span of the rest of the engine.

Some aircraft have a low-voltage warning light to alert you that the alternator is ailing. Some have an ammeter, which is better. Either way, if the alternator fails, the airplane will have power to its radios, lights, and electrically driven instruments only for as long as the battery lasts. And that won't be long. Fortunately the failure of these accessories in no way affects the flight characteristics of an airplane that is not being flown on instruments alone. A student flying in the sunshine just uses his magnetic compass to come on home, and flies as he always did, by outside visual reference. But park it where you mean to leave it—the starter is part of the electrical system, too.

Like any electrical system, your airplane has fuses and circuit breakers. But unlike those in your home or car, these are right out where you can see them and get to them—usually in a row along the bottom edge of the instrument panel. If an electrical problem pops out a circuit breaker, reset it, but do mention this to your mechanic back home.

Again, all this non-sales-brochure information about vacuum systems and electrical systems is no real cause for alarm to a pilot flying in the sunshine. The wonderful J-3 Cub that we all still get misty-eyed over had neither system as standard equipment, and these planes trained the whole second generation of aviators.

The rest of your flight instruments are the *altimeter, vertical speed indicator* (VSI), and the *airspeed indicator*. All three work reliably off the varying air pressures that come through the pitot-static system. With the exception of the altimeter, which has to be reset now and then, none of the others need any attention during preflight.

Press and turn the knob on the altimeter until the hands of this instrument match the field elevation of where you are parked. In flight, set the altimeter by the barometric pressure; this information is routinely broadcast by ground controllers more often than almost anything else.

Altitude settings are not broadcast by FAA ground controllers in terms of thousands of feet, but as inches of barometric pressure. There is a smaller calibrated dial set into a window in the face of the altimeter that you use to match up the correct barometric pressure. Called the *Kollsman window*, this hard-to-read scale is numbered in inches of barometric pressure. As you press and turn the knob to set the correct barometric pressure into the *Kollsman window*, the hands of the altimeter rotate to the correct readout in terms of how many feet you are above sea level.

The altimeter is related to barometric pressure in that it gives us the altitude of the airplane above sea level by sensing the weight of the air mass over it. As you climb, barometric pressure decreases, and a bellows chamber inside the altimeter expands. Through precision linkage, this movement is shown by the unwinding of the hands on the face of the altimeter, reading to higher numbers.

Man, I can't read that
Kollsman window either.

This sensitive altimeter shows 7,200 feet. The Kollsman window is set for a reported barometric pressure of 30.2.

On the ground at Galveston a properly set altimeter would read 7 feet. At Denver it would show an altitude of 5,333 feet on the ramp at Stapleton Airport. Altimeters would be very easy to operate if you could always set them on the ground like a household barometer. But such is not the nature of flying. The airplane is in motion and weather systems are in motion. The changes in barometric pressure in weather systems as they move across the country are described as *high* and *low*, and specific areas within the weather system will be called highs or lows. If a pilot were to correctly set his altimeter for field elevation at Denver in a typical Rocky Mountain high of 30.00 inches of barometric pressure, and confidently fly down to Galveston where a Gulf

Coast low was reporting a pressure of 29.00, his altimeter would show him to be about 1,000 feet higher than he actually was by the time he had flown into the low—and into the ground. The rule of thumb is that about 1 inch of difference in barometric pressure is worth 1,000 feet of altitude, and the sayings that go with it are: "When flying from a high to a low, look out below," and "From a low to a high, clear blue sky."

The *vertical speed indicator* (VSI) works much like the altimeter in that it is connected to the pitot-static system and its needle movement is also calibrated to respond to air pressure changes. But the VSI does not tell you how high you are; it only indicates in feet per minute that you are climbing or descending out of level flight.

The VSI is sometimes called the *rate-of-climb indicator*, and not all trainers have them. You could get the same information by noting on the altimeter that it takes you two minutes to climb 1,000 feet, and therefore your rate of climb is the standard 500 feet per minute.

Your vertical speed indicator shows you are in a 500-foot-per-minute climb—and that's just fine.

The nice thing about a VSI is that along with being as reliable as the altimeter it responds at once to altitude change and the horizontal needle moves upwards promptly to show a 500 rpm climb as you are doing it. The slightest climb or descent moves the VSI needle, and it stays parked at zero in level flight.

The *airspeed indicator* is the last of the primary flight instruments to be aware of, and there could hardly be a more straightforward device. The faster you fly, the more wind pressure is crammed down the pitot tube and through the static system, forcing the airspeed needle around the face of its numbered dial. The airspeed indicator is fairly accurate and reliable for measuring how fast you are flying through the air. The only time it gets funky is at very low airspeeds when the passage of air tends to burble and fluctuate around the pitot tube opening. There is nothing to fuss with on the airspeed indicator, but at higher altitudes it reads slightly lower than it should because the air is thinner. The rule of thumb here is to add about 2 percent to your indicated airspeed for each 1,000 feet of higher altitude.

Light aircraft made since 1945 are required by the FAA to have a standard color-coded marking system on the face of the airspeed indicator. Beginning at low speeds, the white arc starts at the *stalling speed*, or the lowest airspeed at which the airplane will still fly. The top of the white arc is the minimum speed to lower the flaps safely. The green arc is the normal operating range, and the yellow arc cautions you to avoid these higher speeds except in smooth air. The red line is the never-exceed speed. That does not mean that the plane will fly apart if you ever hit redline speed, but it does mean that the manufacturers have washed their hands of you if you go any faster. There is a little bit of unknown reserve beyond all redlines, but don't be that kind of a pilot.

Now we're almost ready to fly. Set the wing flaps for takeoff if your instructor tells you to. Some use flaps on takeoff, some don't. Check the trim-tab indicator to be sure it's in the takeoff position. Even if it's not, in the average light plane you will have to strong-arm the controls only a little to overcome excessive nose-down or nose-up trim—and be reminded of your careless pre-flight procedures. In a big, heavy airplane, wrong trim settings can overcome Mr. America's muscles and eat his lunch for him.

Trainers characteristically have a pin that goes through a hole in the control column and locks the controls. There is a big red metal flag on the pin, and it's all right there in your lap before takeoff. With a little luck you could even get the pin out and controls free with the airplane in motion. But part of your pre-flight should be moving all three control surfaces to the limits of their travel before takeoff. Then for sure you know that nothing is binding the controls.

I don't have a check list in my hand, but this is the last item I can think of, other than being sure the door is shut and window latched and everybody secured by a seat belt, before you switch to tower frequency and tell them, "Two-seven November is ready." Or, if you are at a non-controlled airport, just come on the unicom frequency and say, "Beaumont traffic, Mooney two-seven November is taking off, runway three-zero."

Take one last good look around. Some students are taught at small airports to stand on one brake and use enough throttle and hard rudder-pushing to make the airplane pivot around in a circle, giving you a clear view of all 360 degrees of sky, and ensuring that all the cows and gas trucks are still peacefully grazing off to the side and not ambling out onto your runway.

The check list of cockpit, controls, and instruments seemed to go on forever here—page after page of description—but remember, I was attempting to introduce these items and their functions as if to a first-timer who had no knowledge of the language. I tried to group some of the information together in a use-related sequence.

In real life, unless someone tells you otherwise, go through the pre-flight according to the printed check list for your particular plane. Most of this takes just the flick of an eye, the touch of a hand. Far from being too complex, the pre-flight gets too easy. So will the flying. By 200 hours most pilots pass through their first hazardous period of overconfidence—it has all gotten so easy. To cure at least the pre-flight part of this right at the outset, use the printed check list and say it out loud, touching and saying at the same time as the airline pilots do.

By now, we should be familiar with the anatomy of the flying machine and ready to fly this thing. Let's take off.

11

WHAT MAKES
THIS THING
TAKE OFF?

The takeoff is one of the most exciting parts of flying. First, there is the ungainly rush along the runway as you gently open the throttle to full power, the tendency that all planes have to swerve a little to the left, the mastery we feel in feeding in just enough rudder to hold it in a straight line. Accelerating, concentrating, you can actually feel it when the wings begin to generate lift. And suddenly the airplane is no longer a part of the affairs of the ground; a more subtle yet firm sensation comes into all the controls; the airplane separates from its shadow. You are flying.

But what makes the thing fly?

This question leads us into the rudiments of the theory of flight. I had to go back and read several textbooks for this. For me, it was sufficient that the airplane was willing and ready to fly. Reading the textbooks, I found that there was some conflict and dispute among the acknowledged masters as to the "theory of lift." There is, it turns out, no commonly agreed-upon explanation of why an airplane will fly. I finally went to Dick Collins, my editor at *Flying* magazine, who has written fine textbooks himself and is a careful and cautious man in both word and deed. I explained my dilemma to Collins and he said to accept "whatever makes you feel best about it."

Well, OK. I'll describe the theories of the masters to you in a moment, right after I give you Baxter's Hand-out-the-Car-Window Practical Lesson of Flight and the Function of the Control Surfaces.

Extend the flat of your hand out your car window, palm down. Just sitting still, nothing happens except that you can feel the force of gravity pulling your hand down. Same with a parked airplane.

Now start moving and get some forward motion, some *thrust*, some *airspeed*, passing over your hand, and things start to come alive. First you will notice *drag*, the wind resistance of your hand wanting to drag it back against the thrust. The faster you go, the more drag. Same with an airplane.

Now, with a little airspeed passing over your flat hand, tip the leading edge up a little to form what we call an *angle of attack*. Right away your hand gets lighter, wants to lift and fly upward. Notice that the more airspeed you have, the smaller angle of attack it takes to get lift out of your hand. Same with an airplane.

But at any airspeed there will be a point where if you increase the angle of attack too much you will feel more and more drag and less lift and finally you will feel the wind start to buffet your angled-up hand and the lift will cease and all you will feel is gravity pulling your arm down in the drag.

What has happened is that you have increased the angle of attack to the point where it *stalls* your hand and it quits flying. Don't ever forget this.

Notice that the instant you sort of flatten your hand into the airstream again—decrease the angle of attack—

your hand wants to start flying again at once. So do airplanes.

The hand-game variations can show you how the rudder works. Bend your elbow to a 90-degree angle, rotate your flat, upright hand in the airstream, and feel the right and left *yaw* forces.

If you could get both hands out the window at the same time and twist one upward and one downward, you would feel the *roll* movement that the ailerons give an airplane with one up and one down.

And there you have the basic movements and forces on an airplane in flight: gravity and drag being overcome by thrust and lift; the importance of airspeed and angle of attack; and how the control surfaces affect the straight path of flight through the three movements of an airplane in free flight—pitch, roll, and yaw.

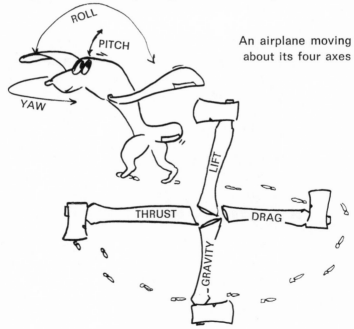

An airplane moving about its four axes

You can even get into subtle sensations of noticing that it takes more control movement at lower airspeeds. And you can imitate the increased lift achieved when the wing flaps are lowered by cupping your hand to imitate the curvature of a wing with the flaps down. Notice this increases both drag and lift and works best at lower speeds. And if you overdo the cupping, as in a Cessna with big flaps fully down, you get more drag than lift and your hand sinks, just like a well-mannered Cessna under full flaps.

After a quick run-through of the Bernoulli and the Langewiesche theories of flight which I have set out below, you will see why I still feel sort of guilty about Baxter's Hand-out-the-Car-Window demonstration and its simplicity.

The FAA *Pilot's Handbook* (which is the text upon which the FAA bases its exam) endorses the Bernoulli Principle, so we give it first.

Daniel Bernoulli, Swiss physicist, 1783: "The pressure of a fluid, liquid, or gas decreases at points where the speed of the fluid increases."

The Bernoulli Principle as applied to the creating of lift in aircraft has to do with airfoil profile of the wing. The airfoil is thicker and more blunted at the leading edge, and tapers in a long teardrop shape toward the trailing edge. The bottom surface of the wing is flat; the upper surface arch is called the *camber*. As the wing is thrust forward with enough airspeed, the airflow passing over the upper cambered surface has farther to go than the air moving straight along the flat bottom surface, so it must move faster to meet at the trailing edge. "The pressure decreases at points where the speed of the fluid increases."

This creates a measurable low-pressure area on top of the wing. At the same time, the air passing beneath the wing is compressed slightly, thereby increasing the pressure from below the wing. Bernoulli and the FAA believe that the combined effect of higher pressures below the airfoil and lower pressures above it create lift.

Bernoulli, FAA, and Langewiesche discussing lift

Wolfgang Langewiesche, master flight instructor, believes differently. He was on our side during the war and wrote a book for the Army Air Force flying cadets entitled *Stick and Rudder*. Both Wolfgang and his book are still in circulation at this writing, forty years later. *Stick and Rudder* is slow plowing to read, but it will teach you more than you ever wanted to know about what goes on with an airplane in flight. To many of us, Wolfgang is the author of the bible of basics. And Wolfgang says: "Forget Bernoulli's theorem."

Wolfgang says the Bernoulli explanation of lift is more puzzling than the puzzle. He says the wing lifts an airplane by pushing down on the air.

Langewiesche bases his theory on the Newtonian law of action and reaction: The wing is pushing down on the air, so the air pushes the wing upward with equal force. Wolfgang sees the airplane's wing in flight as a moving inclined plane, like a surfboard—or a hand stuck out the window of a moving car.

Baxter's Theory of Flight

However you look at this, you can obviously see that there is some inclined plane designed into the way an airplane wing mates to the fuselage. This few degrees of up-angle at the leading edge is the *angle of incidence*. Other than being able to name it, and know that it began in the blueprint stage of your airplane, the angle of incidence is of no more concern to you. It's bolted on, positioning the wing to give maximum lift in level flight.

Design engineer decides the angle of incidence, bolts wing to airframe.

The angle of attack, however, is an entirely different matter. The pilot controls the angle of attack, and the understanding and control of this, combined with airspeed, is the whole heart of the matter of good, safe flying.

The angle of attack is always in relation to the flight path, not the ground. A lightly loaded airplane, going as fast as it will go, needs only a shallow angle of attack to stay airborne. Compare this to a water skier: At low speeds his skis plow along, pointed upward; at high speeds, his skis skim along flat on the surface or at a low angle of attack.

When an airplane in level flight doubles its speed, it quadruples both its lift and its drag. Thus the old Navy

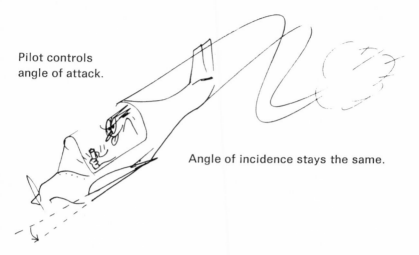

Pilot controls
angle of attack.

Angle of incidence stays the same.

pilot's reply when the reporters asked him to name the three things that had allowed him to live so long: "Airspeed, airspeed, and airspeed."

That's good copy, but a more accurate answer might have been "Airspeed, angle of attack, and *wing loading.*"

The reason for this is that up to a certain point, increased angle of attack will increase the lift of the wing, but beyond an angle of attack of about 20 degrees at any speed the wing will stall and lose lift, and the airplane quits flying. This happens because at too great an angle of attack the wind cannot smoothly follow the curve of the wing. The lifting flow over the airfoil starts to separate and burble at the trailing edge first. You can feel the wheel start to shake in your hand, warning you that the angle of attack is too steep and the wing is about to stall. The more weight the wing is carrying (wing loading), the easier it is to stall.

The cure to a stall is the most basic, yet hardest-to-learn procedure in all of flying: *Release back pressure on the controls.*

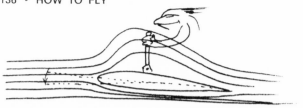

1. Airfoil speeding along, long angle of attack, lots of lift

2. Airfoil at too much angle of attack.
   Shake and burble warns of stall.

3. Idiot keeps stick back,
   increases angle of attack,
   airflow separates,
   wing stalls 'n' falls.

4. Idiot shoves stick forward,
   decreases angle of attack,
   wing fat with lift again.

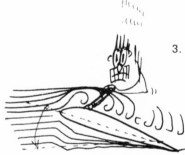

Shove the nose down, give the wing a more shallow angle of attack; speed and lift increase at once and you are flying again.

Human instinct for survival seems to interfere with grasping this basic principle. An airplane stalling with its nose too high is starting to fall. You can feel that in the seat of your pants. The instinct, as the plane shivers and drops, pointing its nose at the ground, is to haul back on the yoke and save your buns. But what you are really doing by pulling back on the wheel is keeping the angle of attack too high and aggravating the stall.

If you just shove the wheel forward and get the nose down briefly, the airplane will respond to this lowered angle of attack by gaining enough airspeed to be flying again almost instantly. Then you can ease back on the wheel and bring the plane back to safe level flight once more.

The best example of speed, load, and angle of attack is to watch an agricultural pilot at work. He takes off with all the load he can carry; he's flying level, but his nose is high. He is plowing along at a deliberately high angle of attack (slowed down by the extra drag) to get the extra lift needed to carry his awful load. Yes, this takes a lot of skill, and yes, ag pilots have a lot of accidents. Not only could he stall the plane by lifting the nose and increasing the angle of attack just a little too much more, he could also stall it from its present flyable condition by making a steep turn. This has to do with increased wing loading in a turn.

The pilot of the heavily loaded ag plane will be making very shallow turns, and here is why. In a turn, centrifugal force adds to the weight of the airplane—adds to the weight of the load the wings are carrying. The steeper the turn, the greater the load. And the pilot cannot see this increase-in-load factor. If the load gets to be more than the wings are designed to lift, the airplane will stall right out of a turn. Not just an obvious straight-ahead stall with plenty of warning from the shuddering wings and vibrating yoke, but one which usually snaps the plane over onto its back, because, while turning, the outside wing is flying faster than the inside wing in the turn. The inside wing loses lift while the outside wing still has some lift. The one-sided lift causes the airplane to do a *snap roll*. Ho boy! The plane does a sudden horizontal spin along its centerline. Not fatal if there is enough altitude left. With the yoke forward, a modern trainer will drop its nose out of such a *whifferdill*, as we call such wild unplanned maneuvers, and enter into a simple recoverable dive. But steep turns are often done at low altitudes by pilots in the landing pattern. And that's bad, because there is no altitude left to recover in.

After Vanneman had taught me stalls, and I had learned to sense and feel the relationship between high angle of attack and decaying airspeed, he asked me if I thought the little old Luscombe would stall in level flight at its top speed. I told him I didn't think so. He asked me then to do a turn as hard and steep as I could. I slammed the sturdy little plane over into a near-vertical bank, yanked the stick back to make it come on around in the turn, and what happened next is a kind of a blur. It stalled, snapped, and spun, right there at top speed.

"You want me to show you that again?" he asked.

"You want me to show you what I had for breakfast?" I replied greenly.

This is not something you have to dread. Flying is not taught that way today, and modern trainers are not as eager to snap the seat out of your jeans as the Luscombe was. But modern trainers, and any other plane, can be stalled out of a turn at well above their normal stalling speeds.

There is usually a graph in the owner's manual which clearly shows how the stall speed increases with the amount of bank in a turn. The graph curve begins very gently, and doesn't turn upward sharply until 40 degrees of bank, and that's pretty steep for everyday flying. In student training you will be taught to make 45-degree turns in perfect safety, so don't concern yourself with lurid images of the airplane dropping out from under you in a turn unless the horizon line is more than 45 degrees diagonal across the windshield.

In a normal 20-degree turn the load factor increases only 6 percent. At a steep 40-degree turn it goes up to 31 percent, and thereafter the curve steepens considerably. In a 60-degree banked turn you are getting close to aerobatic flying and you can feel the *G-load* pressing you down into the seat. The load factor is now doubled, 200 percent. You and the plane now weigh twice as much as you did before the turn.

Here is how much the increased wing load of a turn raises the stall speed of the average trainer:

Stall speed, level flight—48 knots
Stall speed, 20-degree bank—49 knots
Stall speed, 40-degree bank—55 knots
Stall speed, 60-degree bank—68 knots

As you can see, if you were approaching a landing at 61 knots, a safe 13 knots above stall speed, but suddenly stood the airplane on its ear in a tight 60-degree banking turn, it would stall and fall. Steep turns, done low and slow, are to be avoided.

Notice that we have given the airspeeds here in knots instead of miles per hour. At this writing the aviation community is in transition toward a new standard of using the *nautical mile* instead of the *statute mile* for navigation, and knots instead of mph for speed mea-

surement. This practice, long established with the military, has been adopted by the airlines and by the FAA. The changeover is reaching general aviation at last. Part of the reluctance of light-plane makers to speak in knots instead of mph is their inert conservatism; part of it is that knots are always a lower number than mph and sound slower. The public likes to buy fast airplanes. Nobody really wanted to be first to quote slower-sounding cruise-speed figures in his advertising.

It really was an important issue. My theory is that the only reason to buy an airplane is to go fast. Almost anything else is saner.

Old light planes will still have airspeed indicators scaled to mph. Current models have a cluttered dial showing mph on one scale, knots on another. When the transition is completed in a few years they will all read in knots, but airplanes last for decades, so the confusion on airspeed indicators will be with us for a while.

All IFR charts are scaled to nautical miles, and the FAA controllers will speak nautical miles and knots to you, too. But some VFR charts might be scaled to stat-

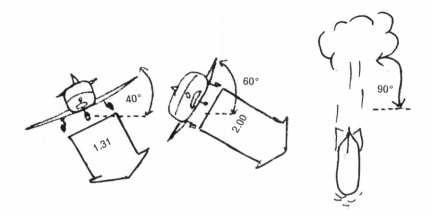

ute miles, so be wary and cautious about knowing which scale is printed on the chart, and avoid some hopeless mathematical errors and navigational mixups that can result from unknowingly figuring knots speed into statute miles or vice versa. I did that once, sitting for my commercial pilot's license. Nothing was working out for me, the clock was running out on me, and after I found the trouble, too late to amend things, I asked if I could just abort this exam. You know, the same way a pilot would abort a takeoff if he suddenly discovered that something serious was wrong. They said no, that I'd just have to flunk the exam and go on home to return another day when I was older and wiser.

Numbers are important in flying. There is a certain number on the airspeed indicator, for example, at which your airplane will be ready to take off and fly. But from your very first day, avoid the fixation of flying just by the numbers. Use all your senses; within the first few minutes of flight you will become aware of the sound and feel of the easy motions of the plane. By its very design today's airplane seeks out safe and stable flight.

You will learn within the first few hours of instruction that you really have to horse an airplane's controls around to get it to do these awful things we have warned of here, such as violently snap-stalling out of a steep turn. One of the most humiliating things that the daring first-hour student learns, after he's shoved the controls around awhile trying just to achieve straight and level flight, is that if he takes his hands off the controls the airplane will do just as well, maybe better. Today's airplanes are designed to, and want to, fly straight and level if they are properly trimmed with the controls in a neutral position. Develop your awareness of the feel and sounds of an airplane doing what it wants to do. This is just as important as getting numbers right. When other pilots speak of a "natural pilot," they refer to the subtle, gentle, physical awareness of that pilot to an airplane in flight. The trait comes to most in less time than it takes to learn to ride a bike.

Now, as to what makes this thing take off. An old flight instructor once told me that the entire secret of flight is a matter of unequal pressures seeking a state of neutral stability.

As you walk up to the parked airplane, it is in a state of neutral stability; the pressures around it are equal.

As you start the engine, the propeller begins to generate enough thrust to overcome the drag of the airplane just sitting there on the ground. It moves forward, thrust overcoming drag.

Aligned with the runway, you give it full power, more than it needs just to taxi. The airplane begins to accelerate over the ground, and the wind begins to flow over the airfoil of the wing. Because of its airfoil shape, and the slight up-angle at which the wing is being presented to the wind, an unequal pressure forms. There is more pressure under the wing than there is above it. The airplane rises, seeking neutral pressure. Lift has overcome gravity.

Because at full takeoff power the airplane has more thrust than it needs just to fly level, it is willing to climb. At cruise altitude you reduce the power. The drag of the airframe now equals the thrust of the propeller, and the airplane will also stop climbing when the power of thrust is reduced. It will seek out its cruise speed and hold steady there, the pressure of thrust being equal to the amount of drag behind it.

And at this constant speed, there will be just enough lift created over the airfoil to overcome the weight of the airplane against the pull of gravity. It will level off by itself, having found equal pressure of lift over gravity.

The airplane will stay like that, in balance of forces, in level flight at a constant speed until something changes.

If you reduce power slightly, drag will slow the plane down to match the reduced pressure of less thrust. The slower airspeed over the airfoil will reduce the amount of lift that the wing is producing, and gravity will draw the plane downward until these forces become equal. Then the plane is quite capable of maintaining a steady, gradual descent, the forces of lift and gravity being equal again.

Had you increased the power instead of decreasing it, the plane would have speeded up at first, increasing its lift, and then slowed down again as it started to climb at a steady rate.

These are the basics of the four forces that affect an airplane in flight. Thrust vs. drag, and lift vs. gravity. They are as much in balance when the airplane is in flight as they were when it was sitting there parked on the ramp.

It's really not all that simple in flight, for there is a

constant interaction between these variable forces as an airplane banks and turns, climbs and dives against the sky. There are endless variations within the freedom of flight, most of them better experienced than read about. Let the airplane tell you, through the sounds and feel of flight.

The first messages will come on your first takeoff. There is always some kind of glory inside me when I feel lift overcome gravity, feel those wings lift. And that's what makes this thing take off and ride the winds.

TWO KINDS
OF WIND

On a windy and gusty day I once asked veteran pilot George Mitchell if he really planned to take off in all that. His classic reply was, "To me the wind is always the same—100 mph over the nose."

What Mitchell meant was that he could manage the plane through the moments of takeoff when it would be affected briefly by the *surface winds*, but once any airplane is flying free of the ground it creates its own *relative wind*, which is simply its airspeed. The relative wind always blows right over the pilot's nose.

Relative wind, always blowing over pilot's nose

In close proximity to the ground, both surface winds and relative winds affect an airplane. They are both the same for an airplane tied down facing a 60-knot surface wind. Surface winds that strong passing over the wings would be experienced as relative wind to the airplane and it would try to lift and fly all by itself. That's why airplanes are best left tied down at night.

Here is an example of how surface winds affect airspeed and ground speed. I was landing a light Aeronca at Galveston one evening. The steady onshore wind from the Gulf of Mexico was 40 knots, which is also just about the touchdown and landing speed of the Aeronca. Flying into this strong headwind and preparing for the tricky business of landing in it, my airspeed indicator read 40 knots. But by looking out the window I could see that my ground speed was zero. I just maneuvered the little plane on down until its wheels touched with no forward speed at all. My relative wind airspeed was still 40 knots.

The tricky part of that kind of landing was that if the wind had suddenly ceased blowing while I was about 50 feet up the plane would have dropped in like a stone. The other tricky part was figuring out what to do with the plane now that it was on the ground in winds strong enough to fly it.

The zero-landing-speed stunt was not novel. There is hardly a little airport in windswept mid-America where some joker has not taken off in a Cub, throttled back to where his airspeed was less than the surface wind speed, and delicately flown the pattern backward. This is only hotdog flying, and such sins have probably wiped out a good many fine old Cubs.

Strong surface winds are a hazard to light aircraft, and part of your training will be how to taxi in such conditions and when not to try it at all. There is no disgrace in going home saying, "Too much wind today."

Aviators always try to take off and land into the surface winds. A moderate headwind helps create enough relative wind for flying speed sooner than if there were no wind; headwind also shortens the takeoff or landing roll.

Airport runways are laid out in directions that favor the prevailing local surface winds, but winds being what they are, they do not always cooperate and blow right down the runway. A wind coming in at an angle from one side or the other is said to be a *crosswind*, and the skill and technique required for handling an airplane in a crosswind is something you will begin to learn on the first day. And if you are like most of us, you will still be learning this ever after.

Once an airplane has put a little distance between itself and the ground, the surface winds are no longer a hazard. In fact, the airplane does not sense them at all, flying as it is in its own relative wind. But the surface winds have an awful lot to do with which way you'll be heading and how long it's going to take you to get there.

I think of the surface winds over the earth as a moving ocean of air into which I have launched my own vessel. If you are a sailor you already know something about being underway in moving currents. But the winds aloft are often much stronger than surface winds, and they blow from different directions at different altitudes.

It is foolhardy to set sail in an airplane without knowing the winds aloft. The asking for and receiving of such information from the FSS goes like this:

"Mooney six-seven-two-seven November needs winds aloft, below ten, destination Kansas City."

"At three [thousand feet], 210 degrees at 15 knots. At six, 270 degrees at 25. At niner, 300 at 35. Surface winds, Kansas City, 180 at 10."

The pattern on this typical day indicates the usual

stronger winds at higher altitudes and the prevailing easterly flow of the air mass across the United States.

Winds aloft are very important to you. If you were flying east at 6,000 feet with an indicated airspeed of 100 knots, the 25-knot tailwind would give you a ground speed of closer to 125 knots. It's also obvious that if you climbed to 9,000 feet and traveled with the air mass moving at 35 knots you would have a ground speed of about 135 knots and be really scatting along. Flying fast, saving gas. Migrating birds nearly always wait for tailwinds.

But lordly and impatient humans will fly in the other direction, bucking the headwinds. Being aware of the winds aloft will at least let you choose a lower altitude where the headwinds will not be as strong in such a westerly flight. Flying west at 6,000 feet will be an exasperating experience: You will be trudging along into a headwind that sets you back 25 miles for every 100 miles you fly forward. Or, in simpler terms, you will have an airspeed of 100 knots, but a ground speed of only 75 when you are bucking a 25-knot headwind.

You can't feel the headwind or the tailwind; the relative wind speed of your plane is the same 100 knots, either way. And the insidious danger is that the flight will take longer upwind and will use more fuel, as if someone had siphoned out 25 percent of your fuel before you started the journey into the headwind.

Knowing the winds aloft will clue you in to the fact that your plane will have a much shorter range when flying upwind. And as you look at the windspeeds at various altitudes, you can see the headwinds are 25 knots at 6,000 feet but only 15 knots down at 3,000. Flying westward at a lower altitude on this trip would give you a ground-speed gain of 10 knots.

Surface winds not only affect your flight in the straightforward business of flying upwind or downwind, but they really add to the confusion when they blow from the side. The main problem here is that a side wind causes *drift* that takes you away from your path of intended flight.

Let's say we are back at 6,000 feet with that wind from the west at 25 knots. Only this time you are flying north, so the wind aloft is from your left. Under these conditions the moving mass of air you are flying through will drift you 25 miles eastward for every hour that you fly north. In an hour's flight at 100 knots you will miss the town you are flying to by 25 miles.

The compensation for this is obvious. You head the plane into the wind at a slight angle. How much of an angle, and how do we determine it? We will learn that later when we discuss cross-country navigation.

13

YOUR
OTHER FOOT

Across the round toes of my favorite rawhide shoes I printed "Shoe" and "Other Shoe" with a black marker pen.

Friends say, "Why did you print that on your shoe?"

"Because it goes on my foot."

"Oh. And the other shoe goes on your other foot?"

"You're a quick study."

"C'mon, why did you do that?"

"Because I'm an old pilot, and old pilots need all the help they can get."

If you look in the cockpit of a big airliner, you will notice that everything is placarded: throttle, flaps, fuel, shoe, other shoe.

Why not left and right? Well, suppose I was facing them? I'd have to figure a reciprocal heading just to put my shoes on.

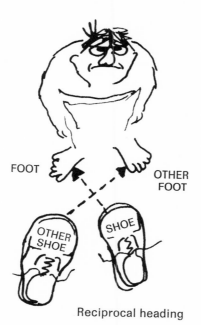

FOOT

OTHER FOOT

OTHER SHOE

SHOE

Reciprocal heading

That's when I decided not to mark them left and right. I always knew that the right was my foot, the left was my other foot. Had been that way all my life. So I marked the right one "Shoe." From then on I knew it went on my foot no matter where I found it. Check list, item one, easily done.

Pilots often have trouble deciding what to do with their other foot. This goes all the way back to the open-cockpit days. You climb up on the lower wing, put your wrong foot in the cockpit first, sit down—and you're facing the back of the airplane. Bystanders laugh.

Knowing full well the old Chinese proverb that a man who teacheth himself hath a fool for an instructor, I nevertheless once tried to teach myself aerobatics in

Got into cockpit with **Other Shoe** first.

George Mitchell's old Stearman biplane. I wanted to learn how to slow-roll the airplane. It's a lovely maneuver in which the airplane departs from level flight and slowly rolls about its centerline like a chicken on a barbecue spit. A slow roll involves a great deal of co-ordination between both hands and both feet on the controls.

The airplane seemed to be going too fast and the events rushing upon me too quickly to be able to sort it all out, recognize what control was to be moved next, find it, and move it in the right direction. Halfway through the slow roll, flying inverted, remembering to keep the stick forward to keep the nose up and at the same time hold the stick hard left to keep the wings rolling on over, and knowing that somewhere along in here some strong rudder pressure would be needed, first one way, then the other, to sustain the nose attitude as the plane rolled through the knife edge of the maneuver—somewhere along in here I would lose track of what came next. Hanging out of the cockpit in the prop blast, watching the horizon roll around, I knew it was time now for my other foot on the rudder real hard, but I couldn't *find* my other foot because during the upside-down part my foot had floated up off the rudder pedal and was now entangled somewhere up under the instrument panel.

The old Stearman, tossing its reins, feeling the lack of firm guidance, roared and moaned and whistled its wires and began to fall out of the sky at odd and unusual attitudes. Knowing I had lost it, and knowing that if I just sat still awhile with the stick forward the heavy end would come on down first, I just rode out the gyrations until I was diving. I could recognize and cope with a dive.

Far below on the ground, George Mitchell heard his fine old airplane groaning through the sky, looked up and saw its wings flashing in the sun, and said to his chief pilot, Earl West, "What is Gordon doing up there?"

And West, being of a taciturn and scientific mind, shaded his eyes, gazed upward, and replied, "How should *I* know, if *he* doesn't?"

Later, in the pilots' room, trying not to slosh my coffee out of the cup, I explained that three-quarters of the way through the roll I lost track of my other foot and couldn't figure out what to do with it.

Your first encounter with the airplane and your other foot will be on takeoff. The airplane will want to swerve left. You may already have your hands and mind full of your instructor's advice about what control inputs you will need to counter the slight crosswind blowing across the runway that day, and now as you open the throttle the airplane responds to some inner urgency of its own and wants to hunt the grass and runway lights over there to the left. The more throttle you give it, the more it wants to stray to the sinister side. Why this? What to do?

What to do is to counter the leftward swing with your foot. Give it right rudder. Give it enough to guide it in a straight line, all the while trying to keep abreast with the rush of events in the takeoff and probably listening to a steady flow of comments from your instructor, delivered in a rapidly rising tone of voice.

Why does the airplane do this when you need it the least? Part of what's going on is *torque*. Part of it is what we call propeller factor, or *P-factor*.

The torque you can observe by having someone gun the engine of your car while you watch the engine. With each burst of power the engine will try to rotate in its mountings. It will heave itself up to the limits of the motor mounts on one side, squashing them down on the other. It only does this with the initial burst of power; under sustained power it settles back down. It was torque that heaved the engine up. An airplane engine acts the same way when you first give it power. But the motor mounts are not as spongy as those of a car engine; the engine is bolted in solidly and tries to rotate the whole airplane to the left a little.

But most of the left-yawing tendency comes from the propeller blast. This is not just a constant cone of wind rushing back from the prop and along the sides of your plane. It manifests itself more as a spiral shroud moving back from the thrust of each blade. The way things work out, the spiral leaves your plane with a final shove against the left side of the fuselage and vertical fin and rudder. This shoves the tail to the right, and yaws the nose to the left. The more power, the more P-factor.

In cruise flight the forces are pre-balanced by the designers, who set the rudder and fin at a slight angle off from the centerline. But on takeoff, P-factor will swerve you leftward. Also, with the continued use of strong power settings as you climb away from the field, or whenever you open the throttle to get climb power, the nose yaws left.

Compensating for this with gentle pressure from your right foot is your first bit of coordinated flying. The control movements of the wheel in your hands will come almost naturally, but teaching your feet to fly will require a little thinking at first.

All of these control movements—stick and throttle and rudder—have to be made in coordination with each other. The airplane will help you do it. It flies a lot happier when it's not skewing along a little sideways; it seeks balanced flight and will mildly resist your getting it into odd attitudes while you are learning.

Another help will be for you to sort out your own cockpit priorities of what comes first.

OK. So you're taking off, concentrating on the footwork required to keep the airplane lined up along the runway centerline. Now the plane is climbing strongly. Your instructor has told you how to reduce the throttle setting to climb power and about what airspeed to keep it at. You are concentrating on holding the nose up just a little above the horizon and the wings level, but the P-factor is at work, yawing the nose a little left.

The black ball in the slip and skid indicator has skidded out a little to the right. The instructor raises his voice above the engine's roar and reminds you, "Right ball, right foot."

Turn-and-slip indicator in a sloppy right turn—

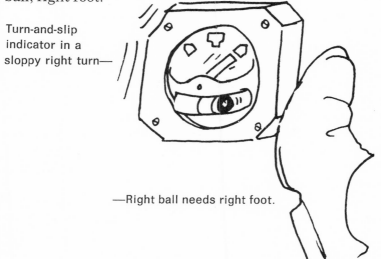

—Right ball needs right foot.

The radio also raises its voice: The control tower is calling your number, wanting you to switch from tower to departure frequency. It is cool in the cabin but sweat is starting to trickle down your temples. All of it is starting to get ahead of you. Who to answer first? This is the time to know the cockpit priorities that are observed and honored by all, from first-hour students to the most senior captain of the line in his bellowing B-747.

You answer the airplane first. The rule of priorities is: Aviate, navigate, communicate. In that order.

Aviate: watch your nose on the horizon line and glance at what your instruments are telling you; push your right foot against the ball to get back into *coordinated flight*. Navigate: look around to see that you are clear of traffic and note which way you are heading. With all that settled down you can pick up the mike and communicate.

If the tower has gotten insistent about "two-seven November, turn left at once," do it. He may see traffic that you don't see. Your left turn is an answer. A couple of clicks on the mike button can suffice for a really crowded moment. At other times you can say, "Two-seven November . . . stand by." Control won't like that much, but it will put him on hold while you do the aviating and navigating you must do before you can communicate. He knows at least that the two of you are in touch. And someday when you call him and *he's* too busy, he'll do the same thing to you. He'll clip back to your call, "Two-seven November . . . stand by." He's not being rude, either. He too has his own priorities in his business, which is basically the separation of moving airplanes. His "stand by" to you is at least his judgment that you are not a part of the problem right at that instant.

If in your judgment the situation is otherwise, remember that the wheels of his chair rest on a solid cement slab and that you are the pilot in command and ultimately responsible for what happens to the airplane. You just aviate, navigate, then communicate.

When you aviate, your senses will instantly comprehend what the stick and throttle will do. The rudder usage is more subtle, but all of it is a part of your new goal of smooth, coordinated flight.

In this initial climb-out your instructor may have given you a typical training-plane climb speed of 90 knots. You are glancing at the nose held a little above the horizon and at the airspeed indicator, trying to nail 90. And about here you will discover that the elevators control the airspeed, and this will strike you as odd because in a car the speed control is the gas pedal.

In the plane, when you have climbed to cruising altitude and are ready to level off, you reduce power with the throttle setting, the nose comes down to level flight across the horizon, and the speed increases some. With the airplane trimmed out in level flight, a reduction of power will cause it to descend; an increase of power will cause it to climb. The *throttle* is the primary climb control.

So we tell you. And you as a student, sitting there trying not to overcontrol the airplane and keep it level, will feel it dive or climb every time you move the wheel forward or back.

Believe it. The wheel (elevator) is the speed control. Go on, pull it back. After a little bit of initial zoom climbing the plane will quickly slow down, in a nose-up attitude. Hold it like that long enough and the airplane will run out of airspeed and stall. Shove the wheel forward to regain flying speed at once. Or push the wheel forward out of level cruise and hold it there. True, the nose will go down and the airplane start to descend. But hold it like that long enough and the airspeed will build up to redline. As the build-up of airspeed creates more lift over the wings it will take increasing pressure against the wheel to keep the accelerating airplane from climbing.

It is, admittedly, an oversimplification to say that the wheel is the primary speed control and throttle the primary climb control, even if you do know that with the throttle closed the airplane is going nowhere but down. The practical truth of this matter lies within the coordinated use of both stick and throttle, because in flight all four forces are always in play: the forces of thrust overcoming drag to create enough lift to overcome gravity. (In most light planes, we are confined to about a 20-degree up-angle of attack, because that's all the thrust we have in our engines.)

I think one of the reasons old fighter pilots never fully regain their senses is that they flew airplanes that had more pounds of thrust than their jet fighters weighed. They could just pull back on the stick, point the plane straight up, open the throttle, and stand it on a column of thrust going straight up against gravity until they ran out of sky. Must be a helluva experience.

The rudder is one of the least understood and most often neglected controls on a modern light plane. Unlike the rudder on a boat, the rudder of an airplane does not actually turn the plane except when it's taxiing along the ground. In flight the rudder can only yaw the nose of the plane to the left or right; *ailerons* make an airplane turn in flight. The rudder only helps the ailerons—sort of cleans up the turn and is used in coordination with the ailerons. When the control wheel is turned left or right, one aileron goes up, the other down. This asymmetric change of the airfoil, out near the wing tips, causes the airplane to roll, or bank into the direction you turn the control wheel.

An airplane must bank to turn.

Orville and Wilbur Wright are generally credited with first having understood that a flying machine needed roll control to make safe turns. Asked by later historians how they knew so much about this, the Wrights are said to have replied, "We were bicycle men first. We understood that one must bank to turn." In their birdcage airplanes, the Wrights successfully experimented with and applied to good use just about all there is to the basic flight dynamics of today's sleek modern trainers. Dick Collins, my editor at *Flying* magazine, may have said it best in his wry observation, "Orville and Wilbur already invented all the magic." There is no magic in the aileron action of banking a plane into a turn. You turn the wheel left, and the left aileron moves upward, spoiling some of the lift of the left wing and causing a downward push in the airflow. At the same time the right aileron moves downward, giving a high-lift profile to the right wing, projecting down into the airflow, giving an upward push to the right wing. The airplane, rolled off balance, starts turning left seeking stability.

But now the unseen force called *adverse yaw* comes into play. Adverse yaw is an unwanted opposite turning force. The plane is trying to bank and turn left, but that right aileron, producing more lift, is also producing more drag. With unequal drag from its wing tips, the nose of the plane adversely yaws to the right as the plane is turning left. An opposite turning force has come into play. The airplane will still turn, but in a sloppy way, skidding toward the outside of the turn. Use a little left rudder pressure to counteract this adverse yaw; use the rudder to yaw the nose back around in a *coordinated* track. The rudder helps the plane turn, and stops the outward skid.

If you push too much left rudder into a left turn, it

will yaw the nose too far left and the airplane will *side-slip* toward the inside of the turn. Such *uncoordinated flying* is called *cross-controlled* and is at times done deliberately to perform the useful sideslip maneuver which we will describe more fully where it's most often used—in landings.

The elevators are also used in helping an airplane through a coordinated turn. The centrifugal force of even the most gentle turn increases the weight and wing loading. Coming back on the wheel slightly increases the angle of attack, creates the additional lift to offset this additional pull of gravity. In a well-coordinated aileron-rudder turn you will see the nose start to sweep across the horizon, but then begin to sink below it. A little back pressure on the wheel lifts the nose.

So all three controls are involved in subtle, coordinated use when making a level turn:

1. The ailerons bank the plane and start the turn.
2. The rudder corrects for the adverse yaw.
3. The elevators keep the nose level on the horizon.

When an airplane is pulled around steeply in a glorious bank of 45 degrees or more, the rudder and elevators trade places in their function and you will be using elevators to stop yaw and the rudder to hold the nose up. By the time you are advanced into doing steep turns this complex-sounding control movement will come from you as an unthinking response to your sensing what the plane needs.

The gentle right and left turns that you will be learning in the first hour are such good and total exercises in the art of coordinated flying that this is the first practice flying I do when I have been away from airplanes too long. I go out and do shallow S turns over a highway, both lording it over those poor motorists down there and using the straight road as a reference line until the feel comes back and I don't have to look at the instruments to know that the ball is centered in a coordinated turn.

Another good skill-building exercise, and a technique that you will be taught during those first hours of dual, is called *slow flying*. The name describes the deed. The object is to see how slowly you can fly the airplane without losing altitude or simply losing control.

To enter slow flight, reduce the power setting while gently coming back on the yoke to prevent the initial nose-down tendency. Do this fairly high up, at some easy-to-see altimeter reading, like 4,000 feet, because you will be glancing at the altimeter often to see that the plane is not descending. It will begin to slow up and fly a little nose-high at an increased angle of attack.

Just keep reducing power and gently increasing back pressure on the controls until the airplane is wobbling along on the edge of a stall, but still holding altitude. The value of slow flying is that all of the airplane's control responses will be exaggerated, and your reaction to them will be accentuated. All this will be taking place in a sort of slow, quiet waltz-time so you can concentrate on what's happening. Nothing is going to happen very suddenly. At the worst you will gently stall it going straight ahead, and the nose will bob. Release back pressure on the controls, the nose will dip down, regain enough flying speed, and resume slow flying. Only a rough, abrupt control movement will get you a rough, abrupt response; it may stall.

After the stall break, apply enough power to slow-climb it back up to 4,000 and try to hold it there. The airplane will want to sink, to lose altitude, while staggering along with its nose slightly up. This is a mode of flight called *mushing*—another self-descriptive term. With just enough power it will mush along in level flight, without losing altitude.

During this exercise the controls will lose their customary tautness. It will take more aileron, more rudder, more elevator movement to feel any effect. The control surfaces, moving in a greatly reduced airflow, will feel loose, just as they do when you flare out from approach and hold an airplane just off the runway when you are going for a full-stall landing. At 4,000 feet you don't have to worry about bouncing it off the cement while getting used to how it behaves in slow flight.

After you master slow flight straight and level, try left and right turns. In this exaggerated control-response condition all the aerodynamics about which we have only theorized will suddenly come to life in your hands. You will feel the aileron sluggishly lift the wing and start the turn; the adverse yaw will swing the nose in a wrong-turning direction distinctly enough to wake up your other foot on the rudder. You will be making cautious shallow turns—an abrupt control movement or a steep turn would stall it, dump the lift from the wings right now—but you can sense all of that. The airplane will again try to sink below 4,000. Add a little power to correct for the loss of lift in the turn.

To go muttering and mushing along in the almost clownish attitude of slow flight at a safe altitude is learning to manage the plane at the very outermost limits of its envelope of performance. Doing this close to the ground would be foolish, because you have only marginal control of the plane. If you lost it, the plane would need a few hundred feet to fall through, controls forward, power added, to regain safe flying speed. At 4,000 feet or so it's OK to lose it—in fact, it's good practice in feeling out what the airplane can do. "If we show you everything an airplane can do you will like it better . . . and get sick," said Vanneman, speaking of slow flight, aerobatics and all.

In slow flight there is no doubt that added power will make the plane climb, or that increased back pressure of the yoke will slow it down. You can play with angles of attack, and with the hidden loss of lift forces in a turn that you may not detect at regular cruise speeds. And all of this takes place at a slow enough sequence that you can separate it and understand the causes and effects in your hand and mind.

When I am checking out in a strange airplane I always ask my check pilot if I may take it to altitude and slow-fly it awhile. There is no surer way of learning any henhouse ways the airplane may have, or of the airplane learning how ham-handed I may be.

You sense the feel of what the airplane is doing mostly just from sitting in it. That's where the old term "seat-of-the-pants flying" originates. If your turn is uncoordinated—slipping or skidding—your buttocks get the uncomfortable feeling of moving sideways in the seat.

However much help the ailerons need from the rudder to get an airplane into a coordinated turn, it will need that much or a little more help to roll it back out into level flight again. Some modern trainers have so cleverly designed the hinging of their ailerons that adverse yaw is almost eliminated and you can roll them in and out of gentle turns with your feet flat on the floor. But John Wayne wouldn't have flown like that. He would have both boots in the rudder stirrups and be flying in a wholesome American way and not go sliding around corners.

After years of happy flying with both lazy feet on the floor I went out to get my glider pilot rating. Gliders, with their long slender fuselages and wings, are very sensitive to adverse yaw and pitch forces. I quickly found out that my feet had forgotten how to fly when George Metts, my instructor, began to teach me how to be towed aloft in the glider behind a tow plane. Anxious to look good for this old friend and former Delta Airlines pilot, I was frantically jockeying stick and rudder back there in the prop wash of the tow plane. Metts had given me as a point of reference the bald spot on the back of the tow plane pilot's head. The more I overcontrolled, trying to keep this hairless vision centered, the worse things got. Finally Metts leaned forward and whispered in my ear (you can whisper in gliders), "You could do about twice as good with half as much of all that."

Thus it will always be with the student, learning co-ordinated flying. You will grow out of overcontrolling quickly, but if you fly much in a well-designed modern plane that has little adverse yaw and get into the lazy habit of flying with your feet flat on the floor, then you will find that you have not made yourself a good-footed rudder pilot. And when the time comes when you really should use the rudder, you will have forgotten what to do with your other foot.

TO LAND
IS TO TRY
NOT TO LAND

Whole books and hundreds of magazine articles have been written on the art and science of landing an airplane. But in my own pasture-pilot experience, the chapter heading here—"To Land Is to Try Not to Land" —is the essence of the entire matter.

The airplane is brought low over the runway and delicately held off as the speed decays, and then just as the lift of wings can no longer support it, the airplane settles those last few inches to be supported by its wheels.

To me, this delicious final touch is the best part of flying. I still think of the landing at the end of a flight as a pilot's signature to his work, and there are few John Hancocks. Many aircraft accidents, although not the most serious, happen during landing. There is an old saying from the other face of flying: "Any good landing is one you can walk away from."

In truth, a good landing is one in which the airplane touches down in the first third of the runway, at the lowest possible speed, with no sideways drifting as the wheels touch.

Any good landing is one you can walk away from. . . .

Landing begins with the descent from cruise altitude. We reduce power, the nose drops, the descent begins. The pull of gravity is now replacing the thrust of the engine to maintain flying speed. Ever planing downward, we swap altitude for airspeed. Yoke forward will increase airspeed, but steepen the angle of descent. Airplanes will fly as well being glided down with the engine idling at zero thrust. A shallow glide is a quiet, dreamy, and peaceful way to descend from the skies, but not always a good thing to be doing to the engine.

The word of caution here is *supercooling*. Throttled back from its labors and exposed to the cool higher altitudes, an aircraft engine will cool off rapidly and unevenly. This sets up stresses within the engine and will shorten its life, and usually foul the spark plugs. Nothing you will be aware of just then, but something we try not to do to airplane engines. Run the engine with enough reduced power to keep it warm, or give it a little surge of power now and then during any prolonged glide.

This short burst of power, also used on long landing approaches, is called "clearing the engine." One of the few times that an airplane engine might just quit cold on you is if you were to open the throttle abruptly after prolonged idling. Wake them up gently.

And always glide with the carburetor heat on, for the reduced power and lower temperatures set up ideal conditions for carburetor ice to form.

Now we have set up two insidious hazards to nag the back of your mind during your long, beatific descent back to earth. And that's so utterly typical of flying.

Not everyone is enchanted with the softly soaring aspects of reduced-power descent. When I proudly took my mother aloft on our first flight together and came back on the throttle to bring us back down to earth again, ole snoozing Mom sat bolt upright in her seat and commanded, "Turn that thing on again!"

"But Mom, this is the only way we can come down and land."

"I don't care. I don't like it. Turn it back on."

Diving back to earth again with Mom and the engine at cruise power would have put us over the airport fence at about 190 knots, and it would have taken two counties to land that thing in.

To me this final approach glide down to the airport is one of the most welcoming views in the world. I think airports are pretty anyhow—the bucolic meadows of country airports, dappled with the shadows of passing summer clouds; the abstract, geometric art of the gray city airports. At night the yellow runway lights in their narrowing parallel are mysteriously beautiful. I'll also admit that maybe all this mooning about how good an airport looks from up there on approach may be just relief at having found the place again.

This is a time when I always settle back in the cockpit with a contented sigh and rummage around some, tidying up the place. Maps folded and put away, check list at hand, toes curled over the cool rudder pedals, ready for the quick and exacting work ahead, but shoes and socks safely tucked away, cracker crumbs brushed off my lap.

An aside here on cracker crumbs. Pilots flying cross-country are nearly always hungry, because the trip took several hours, and there was no place to eat at the other airport, except those vending machines full of peanut-butter-and-cracker snacks. Dr. Owen Coons, aerospace medicine specialist of Dallas, told me that fate could hardly have been kinder to the vagabond pilot. The cracker snacks provide protein in the peanut butter, a slow release of a little sugar from the carbohydrates of the crackers. Avoid the energy zoom of cookies and candy. Cracker snacks, the one food available to the transient pilot, are good for you.

A good landing is built on the orderly and unhurried procedures of a good approach. Although an airplane is capable of three-dimensional movement, and pilots are traditionally free and unfettered souls, there is nothing about swooping down upon the airport from a different direction and altitude each time that is conducive to the neat and orderly landings that we all crave. Even at uncontrolled airports a standard landing pattern with repeated and predictable distances and altitudes is the better way.

At controlled airports the standard landing pattern is mandatory. Landing patterns were the first step toward safety and saneness as airplanes came in from the trackless skies and all tried to line up for the one single track they were going to land on.

The basic legs of a landing pattern are flown at a prescribed height and distance, as shown on aeronautical charts or told to you by the instructor. Each of the four sides of a landing pattern has its own name.

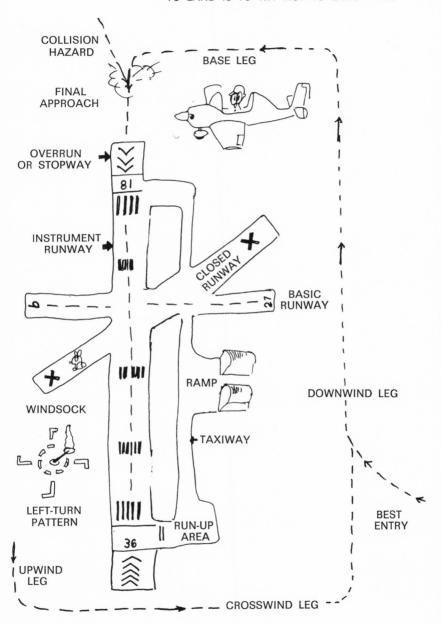

COLLISION HAZARD

BASE LEG

FINAL APPROACH

OVERRUN OR STOPWAY

81

INSTRUMENT RUNWAY

CLOSED RUNWAY

9

27

BASIC RUNWAY

RAMP

DOWNWIND LEG

WINDSOCK

TAXIWAY

LEFT-TURN PATTERN

RUN-UP AREA

BEST ENTRY

36

UPWIND LEG

CROSSWIND LEG

Flying parallel to the active runway and into the wind is called the *upwind leg*. Turning and flying across the upwind edge of the airport is called *crosswind leg*. Turning and flying downwind, parallel to the active runway, is called the *downwind leg*. The next turn, flying across the downwind edge of the airport, is the *base leg*, and the turn and lineup with the active runway and approaching it to land is the *final approach*.

Traffic usually joins the landing pattern by blending smoothly into downwind-leg traffic at the same altitude. At controlled airports traffic is often joined on the base leg, and sometimes aircraft are cleared to land on a long, straight-in final with no pattern flying at all.

The greatest danger of a midair collision is in the landing pattern, particularly where incoming traffic enters the landing pattern. At a controlled airport the tower will be keeping aircraft separated, but the final responsibility of see-and-be-seen rests with the pilot. At a small uncontrolled airport, never assume you are alone. Talk on the Unicom frequency, whether the little airport has two-way radio or not. Say, "Beaumont traffic, Mooney two-seven November is turning final for runway one-two."

More than once have I done this, feeling a little silly talking to myself, and heard the ghostly voice come out of the empty sky, where a local silver Cessna was hidden against a silver cloud, say, "I see you, Bax, Cessna nine-four Quebec will be number two behind the Mooney."

Always be alert, head swiveling, especially when turning from base to final. Level the wings a moment and peer around before any turn, landing or taking off. Often airplanes can be unknowingly close, flying in each other's blind spots. A classic example was on final in a little Cessna one day. Blind to whatever might be above this high-winged monoplane, I glanced downward and saw two shadows racing toward the fence. Even as a low-time pilot I knew that an airplane casts but one shadow, so I promptly turned left and got off the approach. It was a low-winged Piper Cherokee settling down above me. He could see everywhere but down.

The act of flying an airplane will soon become second nature, but no matter how long you do it, a good approach and landing will always require your intense concentration.

Your instructor will fly you through the landing and approach the first time or two, saying, "Follow me through," which means to rest your hands and feet on the controls with him and observe the movements. But do more than that. From the time the two of you enter the downwind leg of the pattern, notice his speed and altitude, notice about how far he's spaced away from the airport. It's a good practice to find some landmark so that when it's your turn you can locate this same road or fence row and fly along it as he did.

Notice at what point he pulls out the carb heat knob, then closes the throttle and sets up his glide. A real artist begins the glide on downwind opposite the point at which he intends to touch down after his long, gliding, square-cornered U-turn, from downwind to base leg to final.

Also notice how the fields or freeways look from this altitude. This kind of mentally stored data will come back to aid you subconsciously when you are approaching some strange airport for the first time. Airports vary widely in their appearance and size, and there are illusions. To even an experienced pilot an extra-wide runway looks shorter, and a very narrow one appears to be longer. But parked cars always look about the same size, ordinary single-story buildings have 8-foot-high walls, parked planes and airport fixtures tend always to look the same. Trust that little range finder that consists of a triangle made up by the distance between your eyes and the distant point you are guessing at. With remembered known objects as reference points, the computer of your mind can come awfully close to telling you exactly how far away things are.

I once flew with a student who kept mumbling numbers to himself and was flying a terribly awkward pattern. When I asked what he was saying under his breath, he told me that he was making his turns by compass headings—that he was flying downwind at 300 degrees because that was the reciprocal of the 120 degrees of the active runway, and that he was now subtracting 90 degrees from 300 in order to fly the proper base leg heading of 210 degrees. I don't know who taught him all that, but good grief, man, you don't need precision airways navigation to fly around the edges of the airport. The thing is lying there right outside the window. All you've got to do is turn your head, look at the active runway, and fly along beside it downwind. When you think you have glided about far enough out, turn and start your base leg. When you see that you are nearing the centerline of the active runway, turn again toward it.

If you were to try to write a textbook on how to enter a room, see a chair, and decide to go over there and sit down in it, the book would be inches thick and readable only by physicians who could understand the visual, mental, and muscular coordinations involved. But few people miss a chair or slam their buttocks into it upon landing after they have had a little practice. Landings are just as much a human movement.

Landings will occupy most of your first hours before solo, and the last hour I have in my logbook of *touch-and-go* landing practice was about a month ago. We call landing practice touch-and-go as opposed to full-stop landings. The British, who invented the language and are sometimes still better at it than we are here in the colonies, call the same thing a more descriptive "bumps and circuits."

Landing is a learned skill. It is one of the times when the designed-in stability of the airplane, its ability to fly itself, can't help you much.

Most instructors teach you to get the plane into landing mode while you are still out on the unhurried downwind leg of the approach. Apply carb heat, throttle back to establish an 80-knot glide, lower the first increment of flaps, retrim the airplane to fly hands off. All small, gentle movements.

The use of flaps—how much, when to apply—will vary with wind conditions, length of the field, and whether or not you are too high or too low on approach, and with the personal beliefs of your instructor. Before you go to fly your check ride with the FAA you will know how and when to land with full flaps, partial flaps, or no flaps. None of this is difficult. It will be an easy add-on skill once you have mastered the basic techniques of landing the airplane.

Once you have made the turn onto final approach, there lies a beautiful view before you. It is an unhurried time. Keep it that way. Even if you are final to Chicago's O'Hare, during those few moments when tower has said, "Two-seven November, clear to land," the airport belongs entirely to you. An airplane landing is more pregnant with its business than the other traffic.

But don't be silly about this. If a giant B-747 is moving out into your landing path at O'Hare, or if a cow and a calf wander out onto the grass strip at home, be mentally prepared to give up the landing and make a *go-round*. Open the throttle, close the carb heat, and as airspeed increases begin to milk the flaps back up in slow increments. Don't dump the flaps. Snatching that much extra lift out from under the wings will cause the plane to settle a bit.

Once you are established on final approach, snug the seat belt down and enjoy the view of the airport rising to meet you. That is the illusion you get; that the airport is rising up to meet you. At this moment there is much valuable information coming to you through the windshield. Look at the spot where you intend to touch down. If it appears to be moving downward through the windshield, then you are too high and are going to overshoot it. If the landing spot appears to be moving upward in the windshield, then you are too low on your approach and your present glide angle is going to land you short of the threshold. Add power. Always add power if you are too low. "Never stretch a glide" is one of the mottos of aviation important enough to be framed and hung on the wall.

Aim your approach at the centerline of the runway. If there is a crosswind to correct for, you will get an early indication of its direction and force by how much the crosswind drifts you away from the centerline.

There are two ways of correcting for the crosswind. One is called the crab angle approach, and the other is to sideslip.

Sideslipping is a deliberately uncoordinated maneuver, but a pretty one nevertheless. The crosswind is drifting you away from the centerline. Lower the upwind wing with the ailerons; the airplane will start to turn into the wind, but give it some opposite-side rudder to stop the turning movement. With one wing drooped, the airplane will begin to slip into the flow of the crosswind sideways, at enough of an angle to offset the wind drift and track the centerline.

The nose may not be aligned with the centerline, but your flight path will be. The airplane, no longer streamlined in the direction it's going, will be a little broadside, and you will be looking at the centerline out the corner

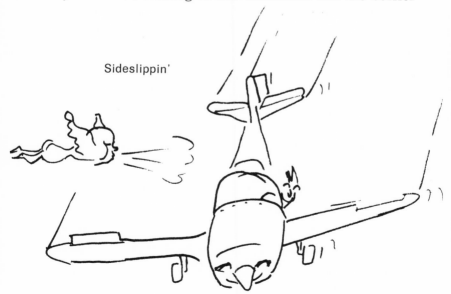

Sideslippin'

of the windshield. Extra drag will cause the plane to both slow down and come down. Sideslips are as useful for descending without speed buildup as they are for drift correction in a crosswind landing.

Of course the slip, carried right down to touchdown, would present the wheels to the surface drifting sideways, and that is not one of the marks of a good landing; it's not very good for the landing gear, either. The main wheels of an airplane have a very high load factor for hard landings rolling straight ahead, but cannot stand as much of the stress of sideways shear loads. So it's necessary to roll out of the slip before touchdown, and get the wings level and the fuselage lined up with the runway centerline.

The plane responds promptly to coming out of a slip —it seems to be relieved to streamline itself again. You can slip safely right on down close to the ground, then get level and lined up with the runway. The art is to touch down quickly before the sidewind can begin to drift you again.

During the landing roll-out in a strong sidewind it's good practice to turn the wheel into the direction of the crosswind, the actions of the ailerons helping to keep the upwind wing down as the crosswind tries to get under it.

The other way of correcting for a crosswind on landing is to simply make a wings-level, "crabbing" approach. Fly at a corrective angle into the wind, exactly as you would on a cross-country flight (see Chapter 16). This is more often the way that heavy jet liners are landed in crosswinds.

I had always preferred sideslips because I learned to fly before trainers had flaps. I first saw the crab approach used when I checked out the diminutive Jean Haley in my own Mooney. Only 5 feet tall, Miss Haley is one of the most determined of women pilots and worked her way up through the ranks of professionals and against prejudice to become a pilot for United Airlines. On her way up, she flew night mail alone and in thunderstorms in cranky old Beech 18s, a prewar-design, tail-dragging twin with big radial engines. Haley learned more secrets from landing hard-to-manage airplanes than most men trained in later years will ever know.

She brought my Mooney in to land in a brisk crosswind, wings level, crabbing it into the wind. Then she simply straightened out the crab angle and touched down, rolling straight ahead, just as she'd land a DC-8. Again, the secret is to straighten out the crab angle and touch down promptly, rolling straight ahead before the crosswind can begin to drift the plane again.

Either way, crabbing or slipping, or even a combination of both, will handle a crosswind landing and be a part of the finesse that will fill up your logbook with so many hours under the notation of "touch-and-go landings."

In addition to dealing with crosswinds, an airplane on final approach may also have to cope with some up-and-down winds: updrafts and downdrafts, caused by convection currents and by the eddies of wind passing over objects near the runway. Vertical air movements, unlike crosswind drifting, come and go rather quickly and are not sustained in effect or result. Coping with them requires quicker reactions to quicker effects.

There is nearly always a downdraft on the other side of a tree line or a steep hill or bluff. Most times you bump through it unaware, your mind involved in the coming touchdown. But sometimes a good downdraft can steal a sudden 25 feet or so right out from under your britches, and if you are down to 100 feet when it happens, reach for the throttle to buy back the altitude loss with power.

Another squirrelly wind effect close to the ground is caused by eddies which roll around buildings set near the runway. The more wind, the more disturbed air. To envision what's happening, just imagine that the moving ocean of blowing air across the field is water. Like water passing over rocks in a stream, the air piles up on the upcurrent side of buildings and makes eddies and swirls on the lee side.

The wind off the shops and hangar at Mitchell's M&M Air Service strip always used to land the Stearman biplane for me a few hundred feet sooner than I expected. It worked out OK, though. I was always a little too high anyway, because the power lines spooked me.

Although there are many landing variables yet to be learned about *density altitude*, wind, and weight, there actually is an ideal approach speed from which any airplane is best landed.

The student, having been taught to recognize the symptoms and hazards of getting too low and too slow, tends for a while to land too high and too "hot." One of the old pilot sayings which is not worth remembering is "an extra 10 miles per hour for the wife and kids," in order to justify a too fast approach. If the airplane is going too fast to touch down in the first third of the runway, plan to go around.

The speed and the angle of descent of the approach glide should be fairly constant until the airplane is only a few feet high off the runway. Then begin the delicate and gentle maneuver called the *flare-out*. This is where the descent curve flares out into horizontal flight, held just off the runway. The skill is to be able to sense that the airplane is beginning to slow and settle, to lift the nose a little to increase the angle of attack and get the final vestiges of lift out of the wing, but not climb.

This will slow the airspeed more, the plane will mush down a little as you gradually increase the angle of attack, and ideally the wing will stall just as the wheels begin to roll on the runway. You have held it off, just over the runway, nose up a little, trying to keep it from landing until it lands itself. It won't be that easy to do.

First there will be the matter of you as a student overcontrolling the airplane—pulling back on the yoke too much while there is still a little lift and airspeed left in the wing. This will cause the airplane to zoom-climb a little, leaving you too high to land and about to be too slow to fly.

Under no circumstances should you shove the yoke forward to bring the nose down or increase airspeed, although that is the correct cure for an incipient stall at any other time. Why not now? Because with the plane so close to the ground you cannot react fast enough to avoid a nose-wheel strike. The airplane will pitch down instantly from forward yoke pressure and slam its nose wheel into the runway before you can correct for this. The nose wheel of a little airplane is frail. Not designed to accept heavy hard-landing loads like the main wheels, the nose gear is just a little stalk out there to keep the propeller off the ground while taxiing. It can stand only light blows, and if the first nose-wheel strike doesn't bend the thing, the bounce from the front end of the airplane will send you kangarooing on down the runway out of control and headed for a noninjurious but awfully messy and expensive final stop with the nose-wheel strut folded back and the propeller wrapped around the cowling. All the people who were waiting to use the trainer next will stop speaking to you.

There are two correct cures for flaring out too high. One is to hold the yoke back and add a little power. This will soften the coming thud. The other is to just hold the yoke back and let the airplane settle on down, nose high, and thud onto its main wheels anyway. Plan to keep the yoke back and the nose high through the bounce that will come to follow that. A third corrective measure, if you feel you have flared up really too high, is to just add full power, holding the nose up just enough to sustain level flight, and do a go-round. Just fly it out of the bounce. Close the carburetor heat and go on around the pattern, thinking cool thoughts and trying to get your act together again. We have all done it.

Although your neck will be flaming red, and the cleaners will wonder what you have been doing in your shirt, if you have to fly an airplane out of a hard bounce caused by flaring too late or flaring too high, just remember never to shove the yoke forward in landing. And remember that your instructor and I once went through this. So did Neil Armstrong and Charles Lindbergh. Nobody is born knowing how to land an airplane, and the makers knew it, and you can't hardly damage one if you keep the nose a little high and hit on the main wheels only.

Only the mains are built for landing loads

Along with traffic, crosswinds, vertical currents, and don't-shove-the-yoke-forward-close-to-the-ground, there is one more demon waiting to spoil a landing that looks like it's going to be so good. This one is called *ground effect.*

Ground effect mostly affects low-winged planes. It is the compression of the air flowing beneath your wings as the wings get close to the ground. Ground effect is always present, but most noticeable on a hot day over a white concrete runway when it's aided by rising convection currents. Ground effect feels like an obstinate, unseen, fat barrier of false lift that seems to roll along under your wings and prevent the airplane from sinking on down to land as it should. It won't balloon you back up into the air as will a bounce or a too-early flare-out; it only causes you to float on along, just off the runway, wondering, "Now what?"

The airplane finally settles through ground effect rather abruptly. Ground effect begins at about one wingspan above the surface and increases as you get lower. It is not as noticeable in high-winged trainers because their wings never get that close to the ground.

After an airplane has landed and there is no lift remaining in the wing, the main wheels are now carrying the load, and the nose—the heavy end—will come down all by itself and trundle along on the nose wheel. If at that time because of gusty winds you want to plant the airplane on the runway more firmly, you can shove the yoke forward. This will depress the nose-gear strut well within its design limits, lower the nose a little, which will give your wings a negative angle of attack, and spoil any trace of lift they may have left.

Landings may confound you in those first few hours of dual instruction, but each one will get a little better. "You are passing through the homicidal stage now, Baxter," Gannaway used to tell me by way of encouragement. When you can safely land a plane they will turn you loose to fly solo, but there will be more to learn, perhaps a period of recidivism, complete with third-hour-student-type bounces. It all passes. You get to be good at it and you know it, and that's a nice feeling to have.

A good landing comes out of a good approach. But a squeaker—a landing where the curved path of flight joins this rolling ball of earth with only a smooth roll-on and a "chir-rrrrp" from the tires, one where they turn to you and grin and say, "Are we down yet?"—that comes from hours of current proficiency and intense concentration in meeting the airplane's needs during those last 3 feet or so of altitude. And oh, it's a fine feeling.

ONE WING
IN THE
SUNSHINE

During the 1960s and '70s, Lee "Pappy" Sheffield was manager of Beaumont Municipal Airport. We called it the "grass airport." The place has since been lighted and paved, and Pappy has quietly retired, but he left his legends.

One was that the airport was open to all: to gliders, skydivers, model plane flyers, crop dusters, Sunday picnickers. The only person he ever ran off was a bearded youth who had an American flag sewn onto the seat of his jeans.

And they say that if all the line boys Pappy gave part-time summer jobs, and allowed to fly in his weary old Cessnas to rack up flying time, ever came back at once, the room would be full of airline captains, corporate pilots, and Air Force flyers.

Pappy would not lock up and go home if one of his chickens had not yet come home to roost. He would sit with a light in the window, waiting and listening. As flying grows more expensive and sophisticated, may there always be enough Pappys and grass airports.

But Pappy is best remembered for his advice about weather flying. He always said, "Keep one wing in the sunshine, and keep smiling." And if you asked him for a further explanation, he'd say, "You look at a pilot flying with at least one wing in the sunshine. He's relaxed and happy, he's leaning back enjoying himself, and he's smiling. But you look at that same pilot when he's flown into cloud. He's serious. He's leaning forward over the controls, frowning at the instruments, or trying to see out the windshield. He's not smiling anymore."

This was Pappy's gentle way of telling his pilots that weather-related accidents account for the greatest number of air-crash fatalities. Why does this happen?

Does rain drown out airplane engines? No. Even the smallest aircraft engine can ingest an astonishing amount of rainwater and never miss a beat. The dual-ignition system of an airplane engine is so enshrouded and sheathed in metal that the ignition harness looks more like plumbing than wiring. I've been in rainstorms so severe that it seemed as if I was flying up a fire hose.

The danger is not from the water; it is from reduced visibility. Man is a visual-reference creature. As soon as he stands on solid ground, he knows which way is up and which way is down. His eyes must always have a visual reference to some horizon, somewhere. Put him into something as shifty as an airplane, where the centrifugal forces in the top of a loop will make him feel as if he's sitting down when actually he's sitting "up," and he must look out the window and find the horizon line in order to "understand" his position.

Obscure the horizon line with cloud, rain, fog, and in less than two minutes, without instruments even the best pilot will not know which way is up . . . until he spins out of the cloud base just before he hits the ground. That's why aircraft have all those artificial horizon instruments and turn-and-bank indicators—so they can be flown in weather when you can't see out the window.

Late in your student training, after you've gotten good enough to fly by reflex coordination and no longer have to concentrate on just flying straight and level or making a gentle turn, you will be given a little *hood time* so that you can understand enough about flying on instruments (without visual reference) to get you down through a cloud layer, or make a 180-degree turn to fly back out of clouds into the sunshine again.

The hood is a simple, light piece of headgear that looks sort of like a welder's helmet and limits your vision to the flight instruments. It's hinged at the temples, can be flipped up quickly if you need to see out, and is worn only with an instructor or observer beside you, unless you are cleared for actual instrument flying. Hood time will be a very interesting and valuable phase of your flight training, neither dangerous nor scary.

Flying with your hood on, the airplane will sound strangely subdued. Your senses are all focused down to your view of that small array of instruments on the panel. It's almost eerie, and you will be astonished at the conflicting messages that your body sends to your brain which must all be overridden by an intelligent interpretation of the instruments. The conflict comes from body sensors denied visual references. You can get part of the same effect by having someone twirl you in a swivel chair with your eyes closed, then trying to stand up. The staggering, falling sensation and the illusion that you are still turning ceases the instant you open your eyes.

The condition is called spatial disorientation, and it's caused by the balance sensors of your inner ear, which must function in association with visual references. The human balance system, located in the inner ear, consists of three semicircular canals, each partially filled with

fluid and each reporting on a different axis of movement. This information is sensed by the brain from hair-
like nerve endings within the semicircular canals. When
you abruptly stop turning the fluid sloshes on a ways,
giving a false turning sensation to the brain, which the
eye cancels out by telling the brain you are not really still
turning.

Pilot being fooled by inner ear canal

Flying when you can't see out the window, and being in a plane which can turn freely about all three axes itself, can create some powerful wrong sensations. The only thing you can do to correct for this is to concentrate on those little artificial horizon and turn instruments. The results can sometimes be comic.

It's not uncommon for a pilot to "get the leans." His training and logic tell him that he is flying straight and level as indicated on the instruments. But his deep body muscles are so sure that the plane is banking one way or the other that he may end up flying level, yet leaned way over to one side in the cockpit. In serious two-pilot instrument flying that's when one says to the other, "I've gone vertigo and you got it."

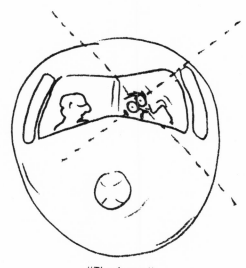

"The leans"
Want me to take it awhile, Captain?

Most experienced instrument pilots avoid a lot of excessive head movement when concentrating on instrument flying. Bending down to pick a chart up off the floor is one of the worst things you can do. The sensation upon straightening up may be that the plane has just snap-rolled to the left, and the pilot may actually snap-roll it to the right to "save" it.

Back in the open-cockpit biplane days, when a pilot was caught on top of a layer of clouds, rather than try to descend through it and get into an inadvertent and unknown-direction spin, he would just pull up, stall it, and spin down through the cloud layer on purpose. The old planes descended at 500 feet per minute in a spin, the pilot knew which way the spin had begun, and you might say that in a sort of wild brave way he was making a controlled descent—hoping all the while for just a quick glimpse of the horizon as he fell out the belly of a cloud.

It is far better to put in a little hood time. But this in no way qualifies you as an instrument-rated pilot. To be able to take off, navigate cross-country, and use the instrument systems to land is a separate art and skill. It is one that I heartily recommend you learn as soon as you are qualified with 200 hours of pilot flight time.

Learning to fly on instruments will take about as many instructional hours as it did just to change yourself from a groundling. To keep his instrument ticket valid, legal, and current an instrument pilot must have six hours of flight experience within the preceding six months. Within those six hours he must also have flown at least six instrument approaches—for that's the dicey part of it, following those needles right on down to near the ground. If an instrument pilot has let his rating lapse (rust would be a better word for it), then he can get requalified by flying with an instructor.

But I do urge that you set a goal of becoming an instrument-rated pilot as soon as you can. Without it, your airplane might as well be a submarine when the clouds hang low. You can't go. With an instrument rating you will understand and utilize all the equipment in your airplane and the magnificent system of charted airways, their aids, beacons, and ground controllers. You will think, speak, and fly more like a professional pilot and fit better into such traffic. Your instrument rating will be the line of demarcation between being a good-ole-boy pasture pilot and being a pro.

Until you become a proficient instrument pilot the best and most valuable maneuver you can learn is the 180-degree turn. A 180-degree turn simply turns you around and heads you back the way you came. The maneuver itself is so simple that you will know how to do it after your first hour of dual instruction. But knowing when to do a 180-degree turn, and drumming into your consciousness the notion that you will do a 180-degree turn if the weather looks doubtful, is something you may have to work on as long as you fly. For those who don't learn this, the National Transportation Safety Board accident reports read monotonously the same: "VFR pilot continued flight into IFR weather conditions." Then they tell how many fatalities there were.

The pattern of these weather-related wrecks, which are probably your greatest hazard in private flying, varies so little that such accidents have earned a popular nickname in aviation—they are called "graveyard spirals."

Here is how it's done:

The non-instrument-rated pilot enters into cloud, fog, snow, or whatever it takes to obscure the horizon line. Within about ninety seconds he is getting false turning sensations from his inner ear. Unable to interpret his flight instruments, which are beginning to twirl before his eyes, and the mounting confusion and panic, he wrestles the perfectly good-flying airplane into a turn. In the turn, possibly in an unknown direction, the nose drops and speed builds up. The pilot, hearing the rising sounds of speed, interprets this correctly as dangerous, but his instinctive control movements are wrong. He knows he's diving, he may even be able to see the altimeter unwinding, so he pulls back on the yoke to pull up out of the dive. In a steep turn this only tightens the turn, gives him a seat-of-the-pants G-load message that he may be pulling up, but since he's already in a steep turn, the up-elevator only tightens the turn and the diving spiral worsens. The pilot realizes about here that nothing is working and the plane has gotten away from him. It is a terrifying experience. If the airplane does not exceed its redline maximum speed and break up in flight, it simply augers into the ground from this graveyard spiral.

During my radio-broadcasting days I worked with J. P. Richardson, the night announcer who was writing songs and hoping to make the big time as the "Big Bopper." J. P., or Jape as we lovingly called him, had reported a weather-related light-plane crash on the ten-o'clock news, and knowing that I was a pilot, asked me why light planes fell out of the sky in bad weather. It's nearly impossible to explain or visualize the experience of spatial disorientation and the graveyard spiral, so I invited him to come fly with me next day so I could show him.

In clear weather, flying one of Pappy's old Cessna 150s, I asked Jape to shut his eyes and describe to me what he felt the airplane was doing. I simulated an out-of-control spiral, which was safe enough while I could see the horizon. Jape said, "We are turning . . . now we are diving . . . now you are pulling up out of the dive . . . no . . . no . . . I dunno."

We had just rehearsed his death, which came just a few months later, after his "Chantilly Lace" became a million-seller, and while he was on tour with Buddy Holly and Richie Valens. They had finished a rock-and-roll concert in Iowa and chartered a Bonanza to get to the next town, next show. The charter pilot had failed his instrument flight exam, but considered himself good enough on instruments to take off in the middle of the night in a snowstorm. The wreck was found about two minutes from the field where they took off. The plane had spiraled straight in. "The Day the Music Died" is the way their death is remembered in song. But I will always be haunted, wondering how much Jape knew and what he was thinking in those last few seconds.

Personally, I still could not believe that a pilot could lose control of a plane just from flying through clouds. My own "born again" experience happened on a brave Texas-to-New York flight when I had precious few hours in my log book. I was homeward bound in a little straight-backed Cessna 150, scud-running beneath an overcast, between rows of mountains, down in the Shenandoah Valley. I knew this was risky, but I had gotten away with flying under low ceilings before.

What I was not paying attention to was the *dew point–temperature spread*. This vital information is broadcast by the FSS along with altimeter settings and wind direction. When the dew point and the temperature become the same, fog forms—as it now did in my beautiful valley whose rocks and hills are so celebrated in song and verse.

I crept lower, until windmills were flashing by, and farmers on tractors were ducking and shaking their fists. There is just no place in this scenic rocky part of the country to force-land an airplane. I considered a controlled crash, stalling in, flaps down. One could survive an excursion through thickets and fields like that, but it would total the airplane. And this is when I found out about the silly instinct pilots have against deliberately wrecking a good-running airplane.

The fog thickened; I could only see down through the corner of the windshield for about fifty yards ahead. But glimmers of sunlight told me that the overcast was thin. As you are doing now, I had read all the horror stories of what happens if you fly into clouds, but I decided it probably didn't apply to me. Anyone could set up a 500-foot-a-minute standard rate of climb; just sit still, and in two minutes the little Cessna should pop out on top in the sunshine like a mullet from a gray pond.

With the cold, deliberate detachment that a suicide must feel as he loads the clip, I set up the climb and entered into the clouds. Why not? I was lost already, mountains on both sides, and when you're scud-running you are usually too low to pick up any *VOR* navigational beacons to find out where you are. The losing streak quickly compounds itself, like a burnt-out crap shooter at the tables in Vegas. So I bet my heap.

Actually it wasn't so bad. It was cool and quiet in the muted cloud—sort of like flying inside a Ping-Pong ball. I didn't move or touch anything. And sure enough, a bright silvery light soon flooded the cockpit. I was almost out the top. I glanced up to see how soon. Moved my head. That did it. Vertigo.

The little Cessna fell into a spin. I had no idea of which way, but they taught spin training in those days, and I urge that you ask your instructor to teach spins to you now, even though this sickening sort of violent maneuver is no longer required in private pilot's training. From my past instruction I recognized the sound of a spin. And I knew I would be dead in less than sixty seconds. Again, the feeling was one of detachment, tinged with regret.

My mind was flashing up all the spin-related events it knew. An instructor's voice came back to me: "The folks in Wichita didn't really want this little airplane to spin easily. That's why if you just cut power, turn it loose, it stops spinning all by itself and goes into a gentle gliding turn."

That was the straw that floated to me, as I was drowning in this whirlpool. I pulled back the throttle, took my feet off the rudders, folded my arms across my chest, and gazed sort of forlornly down out the corner of the windshield, wondering if this would hurt much.

I heard the plane quiet down, slow down, but still had no idea of what it was doing. Then the green blur of earth, and at the same instant we glided out from under the cloud bottom at about 200 feet in an almost wings-level gentle turn. I was alive.

More hair-raising scud running led to a pool of sunlight in the next valley. I got into this pond of light and tried to spiral upward. This is when I learned that a light airplane already straining to stay at altitude during a steeply banked turn just doesn't have enough lift or thrust left in it to climb. I sank to the bottom of my well of light like a gasping, dying fish.

Over the next hill, and flashing by one more silo, there was a long trough of sunlight. It was long enough and wide enough for me to climb in it, wings level, make a steep turn as the wall of cloud approached, then level out and climb like mad again—a pattern similar to an escalator and its level turnaround landings at each floor. I broke out on top, found distant Atlanta on the VOR, and went forth a free man, to sin no more.

Atlanta was in the clear, but I found that I could not remember the two-digit runway number I was cleared to land on, nor translate this information into the required logic of identifying that runway by its compass heading. I flew well, landed well, but seemed to be in a robotlike trance. Atlanta was not as crowded with jet traffic in those days, and the tower gave up on me and said just land on the runway I was pointed at, since I seemed to be landing on it anyway.

I later discussed this incapacity to reason or think with a friend who is a neurosurgeon. He listened to the entire tale, and said I was in a state of delayed shock. It's an extreme condition, just before the screaming state, when a person is confronted with his own certain death. He said the thinking part of my brain had already shut down, and the more primitive motor controls of the old brain were flying the plane well enough.

The horror went on after landing. At a motel, taking a hot bath, I began to think the bath was red with blood and that I was actually back in the Shenandoah Valley, a part of the shredded aluminum hanging from broken, fog-dripping trees. I fled the bath in terror, dressed, and went into the crowded snack bar.

There was one empty stool. I slipped onto it, and neither person on either side made a move. I sat there, and the waitress—busy back and forth behind the counter, friendly, smiling to the others—never even glanced at me in this newly filled slot at the bar.

The horrors began to come back—the spin, that fog-filled valley, me dead in the wreck. Was I only dreaming that I had escaped because I wanted to live so much? Was I sitting here in this café, or in some supernatural nether world?

Then that plump blond Georgia girl finally looked straight at me and said, "May I help you, suh?" She is probably still wondering why the gaunt man with the strange, hollow eyes first offered to marry her, then asked for a cup of black coffee, "and another one every time you see me."

As one who still considers himself as living on borrowed time I urge you to avoid flying into clouds. There are varying rules for VFR flight within part 91.105 of the FARs, but IFR minimums are easy to remember: Anytime the ceiling is below 1,000 feet and the visibility is less than 1 mile, it's IFR. Don't go.

You should also commit to memory the *cardinal altitudes*. Beginning at 3,000 feet above the surface, eastbound VFR airplanes fly at odd thousands plus 500. Example: 3,500 feet. Westbound planes fly at even thousands plus 500. Example: 4,500 feet. IFR-flight-planned aircraft are assigned odd thousands eastbound, even thousands westbound. My prejudicial memory trick for that one: Westerners are even, Easterners are odd.

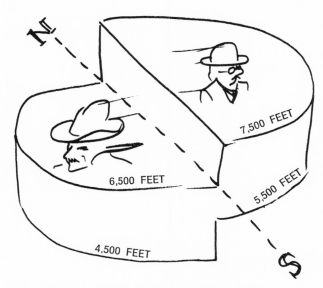

Easy way to remember VFR cardinal altitudes:
Westerners are even +500 feet
Easterners are odd +500 feet

The rules for VFR flying are designed to keep the non-instrument-rated pilot clear of clouds. Within these rules there remains plenty of room for safe and happy flying. The temptation to bust clouds and the rules often comes at about the 200-hour overconfidence level, and at about the 1,000-hour bravado level. The urge behind the tendency of VFR pilots to take chances in marginal weather is so common that it, too, has a well-known slang name in flying: "get-home-itus."

The weather hazard, and the matter of your making judgments about it, begins as soon as you become a solo student. About half of the forty hours of student flying will be solo, and a good part of that will be taken up in making your prescribed cross-country solo flights that we will outline later. The reason these flights are required is to teach you navigation; they are not intended to be exercises in courage. In all of your flying experiences to come you will gain only respect, not contempt, if you cancel a flight because of doubtful weather.

True, canceling can cause a mess of interrupted schedules. So much so that the cynical saying "If you have time to spare, go by air" has risen up among us. But even after I had my instrument rating, I once junked a flight and came home by airliner. The forecast was for galloping thunderstorms, low ceilings, and rain and fog, with a night arrival back home. Single pilot, single engine, night IFR flying into invisible thunderstorms—that's what you could call bad odds. I bought a ticket on an airplane that had three engines, three pilots, and onboard radar for finding embedded storm cells in the night.

"Pappy," I said, "I left your Cessna tied down in Dallas."

"That's the least expensive thing you could have done," he said, even though daily tie-down fees were mounting and we'd have to ferry me back to Dallas to bring his Cessna home when the weather lifted.

Another pilot once said, "I don't fly weather because of my back."

"You got back trouble?"

"Yeah, a big broad yellow streak running right down the middle of it."

Again, the association of risk-taking with courage. Do not let this subtle peer-group pressure that still exists in aviation cloud your own judgment. And from the time you solo at a tender ten or fifteen hours, you will always be making your own judgments about flying. The study of weather and flight planning will be very much a part of your practical and written instructions in learning to be a pilot. Some grouse about this. I take it as seriously as I would take swimming lessons if I lived on a houseboat.

Before a flight, when it's still in the planning stage, go beyond the regular sources of aviation weather information that you will learn about and use both the weather maps and satellite pictures you see on the local TV, and also use newspaper weather maps. You can't ever know too much about the weather.

None of this is to downgrade the joys of just plain old VFR flying. My old friend Duane Cole, veteran barnstormer and air-show pilot from the 1930s, still flies his non-radio-equipped Taylorcraft all over the country to do his graceful and beautiful air-show acts. Duane has written a book, *Happy Flying, Safely* (Milwaukee: Ken Cook Publishing Co.), that stands in sharp contrast to all the excellent books that have been written on weather flying. His book tells how to stay out of weather. And how to fly cross-country with no radio. There is some righteous anger in it, for this veteran pilot, VFR only, has never missed an air-show appointment in over forty years of professional flying—and that includes winning the U.S. Aerobatic Championship once.

Duane believes that the FAA should teach more about how to stay out of weather than how to fly through it. Advice worth heeding. It's worked well for him, although he sometimes leaves a day early. Taken to the exclusion of all else, Duane's book would set scheduled flying back to about where it was in the 1920s. But as a counterpoint, he's worth knowing.

Duane also believes in spin training. He told me that 90-percent of all the pilots who come to his school to learn spins and spin recovery to supplement their own skills would have died in their first inadvertent spin.

You need not be obsessed with the fear of an accidental spin, and most trainers built today will recover from a spin if you just pull the throttle back to idle power and turn the controls loose. Control movements for more prompt and positive spin recovery vary with the type of airplane and how it's loaded. But the general rule is to reduce power, briskly shove the control yoke forward with the ailerons in a neutral position, and apply hard rudder opposite to the direction of a spin. The plane stops its spin, which is really just a stalled condition, enters into a dive, gaining airspeed, and flies nicely out of the dive with enough back pressure on the yoke.

Spin conditions result from too high an angle of attack, and the old cure is still the same: *Get the yoke forward.* Many spins are preceded by all the usual stall warning sounds and buffeting of the controls, but a spin out of a too-tight turn may occur more suddenly. Yoke forward and opposite rudder will stop a spin before it develops.

The government officially halted spin-training requirements for students in 1949. One of the reasons for this action was the high rate of spin-training accidents.

Some say that there was pressure from within the aviation community to omit spin training because it was scaring off students.

The present rationale is that if a student can recognize and prevent a stall he will never come near a spin anyway. There is some controversy over this, the opposition saying that it may even be immoral to be licensing pilots to fly without full knowledge and understanding of all the airplane can do. "For as long as airplanes can still spin, spin recovery should be taught."

There is nothing illegal about asking for spin training, and all trainers are certified by their makers as having good spin-recovery characteristics. I would not spin our high-performance Mooney just for the fun of it, but I did call the factory for a description of the best spin-recovery methods. Glad I did, too. While checking out another pilot I just sat there as he forced the nose up for too long in a power-on stall. When the stall broke with one wing dropping sharply instead of level and straight ahead, I knew to pop the yoke forward, give it hard opposite rudder, and not aggravate the stalling wing by flapping the ailerons. I agree with Duane about knowing how to recover from at least one spin: You won't forget how afterward.

A spin in VFR weather is a wild and exciting experience, better than any amusement-park ride. It's the spin when you are in cloud and can't see out the window that is so dangerous. You can't always tell which way it's spinning, right or left.

An exception to climb-stall spins and turn-stall spins is the one that may be associated with *wake turbulence* from a heavy aircraft ahead of you. In this situation your light plane will simply be tossed over and out of control like a chip of wood in the wake of a passing boat.

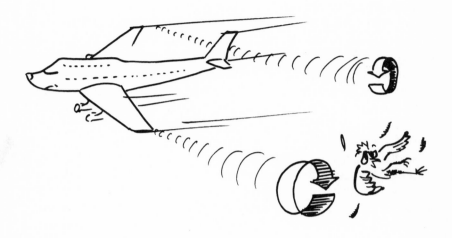

Wake turbulence is caused by the powerful funnel-shaped spiral *wing tip vortices* that form and trail back from the wing tips of any plane in flight. The bigger the plane and the more heavily loaded its wings, the worse the wing tip vortices. Passing through the wake of another light plane would only be a slight bump. Passing through the wake of a jet liner could quickly roll you upside down.

The danger is only present in mixed traffic at big airports, and the safety measures are simple. Stay out of that invisible wake. The pattern of the wake is always the same, and easy to visualize. The twin vortices trail from each wing tip, broadening and weakening with distance. Most important to know is that the vortices slant downward at about 500 feet per minute. If you are level with or slightly above the path of a jet liner, its wake passes below you.

The wake turbulence also vanishes as soon as the wheels of a landing jet pick up its load and the wing unloads. The turbulence may linger a minute or so at the threshold of the runway, but if you hold above his landing path and touch down past the point where he did, you will be clear of his wake.

At a busy big airport the tower may badger you about such a high, lingering landing approach. Remember who's in charge here. Just tell him: "Wake turbulence avoidance." There will be plenty of room to land a light plane beyond the jet's touchdown point.

On takeoff, where light planes are mixed with heavy jet traffic, the tower controller usually cautions you about wake disturbance. At the same time he may be urging you to get going and you feel the pressure of the traffic behind you waiting for you to take off. Again, if you want to tell him you are going to sit there in the number-one-to-take-off slot for a minute for wake turbulence avoidance, it's your fanny, not his. Wake turbulence has never thrown a tower controller out of his chair.

But once again, remember that the spiral vortices begin only after the wing of a jet on takeoff picks up the load. If you think you can get off and be climbing or turning away or staying above his track before the point where the jet rotated up off the runway, then it's safe enough to go.

There are two other unseen "gotcha's" in the sky, even in a friendly, clear sky. Both have to do with altitude. One is *hypoxia*, which will affect your performance; the other is *density altitude*, which will affect the performance of your airplane.

As you know, the air is thinner and there is less oxygen at higher altitudes. Both you and your faithful little engine will be noticeably running out of air by 10,000 feet. The engine will be asking for a leaner fuel mixture to match the reduced oxygen it's getting for combustion. And by 10,000 feet you can be running it leaned back and at full throttle but getting less than 50 percent power. The view is magnificent, but the performance is sluggish.

The reduced oxygen supply to your brain produces a different set of symptoms. There is a wonderful feeling of well-being, of euphoria. Sort of like a glass of champagne on an empty stomach. But at the same time your reactions and reasoning ability will start to decline.

My own test is to try to figure a reciprocal heading in my mind. A reciprocal heading is only the number for the direction opposite the one you are heading in. For example, the reciprocal heading of 360 degrees is 180. But that's an easy one. Try the reciprocal of a heading of 231 degrees. In actual flying I usually cheat and just read the opposite end of the needle. It's hard enough for me to do with a brain full of oxygen; impossible at the edges of hypoxia. The sure clue is when I get to laughing about it.

The Federal Air Regulations dealing with hypoxia are much more liberal than my own:

- Above 12,000 feet for over thirty minutes, crew don oxygen masks.
- Above 14,000 feet anytime, crew breathing supplemental oxygen.
- Above 15,000 feet passengers must have oxygen, too.

This should tell you a little something about how we feel about passengers.

In the pressurized cabin of airliners the cabin altitude stays at about 8,000 feet. During World War II, the Air Corps decreed that we would don oxygen masks at 10,000 feet as we stood beside the open waist windows of the mighty B-17.

Personally, I go by the old Air Corps rule of 10,000 feet being high enough without supplemental oxygen. Part of this is my fifty-seven years, part of it my ever-present old briar pipe. Smokers should assign themselves an altitude penalty of 2,000 feet or more. This rule is not for a pop-climb up to 11,000 or 12,000 and coming down again soon as possible, but for a prolonged cross-country cruise.

After the initial goofiness symptoms of hypoxia comes the feeling of deep fatigue and a dull headache. Prolonged oxygen starvation results in loss of consciousness and ultimately death. The first and last symptom of this stage of hypoxia that you may recognize is a bluish tinge to your fingernails. If you see the pilot dreamily examining his fingernails, get him to come on down.

Density altitude, another made-for-aviation phrase, has to do with the decrease of lift that occurs with the increase of temperatures. The only time density altitude will affect you will be when you are operating out of very short fields or at very high-altitude airports on hot, humid days. Then it will affect you plenty.

Because the air is thinner at high elevations, and the engine develops less horsepower and the propeller less thrust and the wing less lift, an airplane that will take off in 1,000 feet at sea level will need 2,000 feet to get off from mile-high Denver.

Simply doubling the takeoff distance at 5,000 feet is fine—*if* the wind, temperature, humidity, and load are the same at Denver as at sea level. But since such conditions are not likely, let us consider what effects to expect from increased temperature and humidity. Obviously lightening the load and taking off into a good headwind will improve matters, but high temperatures also produce thinner air and, combined with high altitudes, can produce a takeoff run longer than the runways of some Rocky Mountain airports. Adding the temperature factor to the existing altitude problem gives us the figure we call density altitude.

Your owner's manual will have a density altitude takeoff performance chart in it. But the matter becomes so vital at places like Sardi Field, Aspen, Colorado, where the landing pattern altitude is 11,000 feet, that there is a huge sheet of plywood dominating the operations room wall which serves as a density altitude chart. Hourly temperatures are posted on the big chart where pilots can't miss it.

The runway at Sardi is 6,000 feet long, and on a hot humid day you can stand right there in front of the density altitude chart and compute that it will take your airplane 7,000 feet to take off. At a high-altitude airport such as Sardi, the four-place Cessna 172 is used as a two-place airplane. Engines are started with the mixture control leaned more than halfway out. A healthy, lightly loaded Cessna 172 that will bound off the ground at sea level and show you an initial rate of climb of about 1,000

Not the way a Cessna 172 looks—but the way it feels at a density altitude of 10,000 feet and 95 degrees F.

feet per minute will use up all of Sardi Field on takeoff and stagger into the air climbing at only 150 feet per minute doing its very best.

And when the midday temperatures go high at Aspen, raising the density altitude and creating computed takeoff runs longer than the runway, the pilots just relax, visit, wait until the cool of the evening, or leave early the next morning.

Arriving under high density altitude conditions can be a thrill, too. The high altitudes make the airspeed indicator read too low. With full flaps, the Cessna 172, which floats to earth like a parachute at sea level, comes in at 90 knots, barely aloft and sinking as if it were loaded with bricks, and uses up all the runway landing.

Aspen's 10,000-foot-plus elevation is used here only as an extreme example to dramatize the effects of density altitude. But density altitude—that is to say, the altitude, temperature, and humidity—will affect all takeoffs at all airports to some degree.

George Mitchell was watching one of his ag planes get smartly off the runway in a few plane lengths one cold, clear, dry day at his 2,500-foot sod strip at M&M Air Service in Beaumont, where the elevation is 30 feet. "I wish I could bottle up a day like this and save it for next July," he said. For in July, when the temperature and humidity at Beaumont is likely to be 98-98 and you can breathe the air or drink it, his loaded biplanes use up nearly all his runway.

So even at sea level, heat and humidity change the density altitude and lengthen takeoff runs. Density altitude becomes a factor when the three H's are up: height, heat, humidity.

I once thought that wet air was fatter with lift than dry, but it's not so. Water vapor weighs five-eighths as much as the same volume of dry air. The coffee stays in the bottom of the cup, the vapor rises. So does smoke from the fire.

All of which brings back to mind a wonderful story about a brisk and proper English operations officer, stationed in France with a squadron of Sopwith Camel fighter planes during World War I.

The Camel was a feisty little biplane, not easy to manage, and is said to have brought down more British aviators than the German Fokkers did.

The major, clean and crisp in his uniform, left his desk to go fly a bit and maintain his proficiency in the churlish Camel. His subordinates saw him open the throttle, raise the tail, blast away across the field and into the trees. The Camel shed its wings like cardboard on the first row of tall poplars, left its wheels on the bordering road, splintered its propeller on the farm-yard's low stone fence, and tipped high into the air, falling inverted into a pigsty among the swine.

There was long silence, a few clouds of steam, and then the dripping major reappeared, walking with erect dignity through the pathway he had carved, back to his operations office, whereupon he drew out a flight report form and wrote, "There was absolutely no lift in the air today."

He may have been right.

There is one other weather condition that will rob your wings of lift, and that is an innocent-looking layer of frost.

Piles of snow, or layers of ice, obviously deform the lifting shape of the airfoil, look heavy, and should be removed before flight. But frost, just a thin layer of frost, will send you into the trees at the edge of the airport, too. Wipe it off before you fly. Thick dew has much the same effect but wipes off easier, and dries quickly in the prop blast.

The serious matter of in-flight airframe icing is of no concern to you just now, since ice forms only in cloud, and VFR pilots do not fly in cloud, do we?

You will be doing some night flying as a student, unless you specifically request no night instruction, and become licensed as a pilot with such a restriction on your certificate. But there's really no reason to avoid night flight instruction. It's useful and not nearly so dramatic as it first looks and sounds. In fact, some of my most beautiful flights, and the smoothest ones, have been in the dark velvet of night airs.

Night VFR is actually easier than day. Except in the most sparsely populated areas, ground lights and starlight give a clearly defined horizon reference. Taking off from homeplate, the string-of-pearls freeways define themselves in an instant sense of direction for you, and you'll be surprised at how near and clear your rival neighboring city looks at night. Big cities cast up a sky glow that you can see for many miles and give the impression that oil resources must be inexhaustible. The moon and stars race you across the face of every river and pond, and the night air seems so fat and tranquil with lift, the airplane so muted and stable, that I once radioed Pappy that I was going to get out and stroll up and down on the wing and enjoy a good cigar before coming down. Might not even come down at all, said I.

One of the cautions about night flying is to be sure you remain VFR. You can lose horizontal ground reference over wilderness areas where there are only a few scattered ground lights, or if you take off from a lakeside or coastal city and turn out over the water where there is no horizon line on a dark night.

The Navy recently conducted tests with skilled jet pilots to see how much visual reference a human can obtain from a single light in the darkness. The pilot, seated in a darkened room, was asked to report on the movements of the single light within his view. All the reports indicated that the pilots perceived different movements from the light with no other visual reference to relate it to. The light was mounted in a fixed position.

Night distances are tricky, too. One moonlit night, as I was enjoying a cruise over the approaches to nearly deserted Jefferson County Airport near Beaumont, I took evasive action to dodge what I was sure was the landing light of an Eastern Airlines plane on approach. There was nothing on the radio, but I dodged it again before I figured out that I was avoiding the planet Venus.

In the telling of these tales I want to avoid making either the night skies or the day skies ominous to you. The formal study of aviation weather sources and meteorology will occupy much of your time in ground school. The study of weather through the windshield and the steady building of your own experience will become a growing part of your native skill as a pilot for as long as you fly.

Even as the ancient mariner who contemplated the surface of uncharted seas looked aloft and sniffed the air before he cast off from the shore, the study of the skies is a thing of endless fascination to a pilot.

I say "skies," because there may be only one sky above the groundling, but there are many skies to fly through. I have never seen two exactly alike. My secret pleasure is to go find summer cloud castles far from the routed path of airways and to soar and climb and dive beside their silvered ramparts (always maintaining VFR).

Dawn patrols are beautiful, too. We view the sunrise tinted from the top. And a sunset is a pilot's special privilege. His wings are still showered in golden light while far below the earth is being purpled with night.

The experience of the airman's skies was best caught in the words of a child who was a passenger in the Boeing 727 back when my wife, Diane, still flew with Braniff. The jetliner took off and rose steeply through the yellowish city smog and clag, then porpoised out on top, shedding the stuff from its wingtips. As a clear sunlight flooded the cabin, Diane looked down the aisle to see a small boy standing in his seat craning upward to see out his window. The seat-belt light was still on, so Diane went to him, but only asked him what he was looking for.

"The Kingdom," said the child.

But for you, for now, let me only pass along the advice of my airplane partner, Certified Flight Instructor, Instrument, Elmer Lee Ashcraft, who said, "Students should not become involved with clouds."

16

CROSS-COUNTRY

After you have learned to land, and have soloed, and are an aviator, albeit not yet a licensed pilot, at least ten of the twenty hours of solo time you have yet to fly will be spent in cross-country flying. This is using the airplane for what it was really designed for—traveling long distances over the face of this earth, passing freely through the air, unencumbered by the exigencies of land or water travel.

The need for some means of air navigation arose as soon as airplanes were strong enough to fly very far from their launching fields. The first manner of aerial navigation was a natural and human way of doing it, and is still very much in use today. It is called *pilotage*: simply looking out the window, recognizing familiar features of the ground, and finding your way home the same way a cat does.

Things do, however, look different from the air, as you will discover when your instructor invites you to find your way back to the airport from the practice area for the first time and you realize that you are lost somewhere about 20 miles from home. But humans seem to have an uncanny capacity for recalling casually seen landmarks. You will enjoy the quick and natural growth of your skill at pilotage navigation, but it only comes with flying experience.

I have known old pipeline patrol pilots, whose flying takes them endlessly over the network of buried pipelines, following the cleared rights-of-way, looking for leaks. Such pilots seem to have memorized how the entire southern United States looks from the air. I think you could put a paper sack over their heads, fly them out anywhere, unbag them, and they could still take you home.

Following pipeline or power line rights-of-way, freeways, and railroads is a form of pilotage, not freely admitted perhaps, but still as much a nav-aid as in the days when IFR also meant "I Follow Railroads."

The compass was the first navigational instrument to be added aboard the flying machine as pilots stretched their range. Pilots use the compass just as sailors do in navigation at sea. This form of navigation is called the same thing on ships or planes—*dead reckoning.*

Dead reckoning requires only a compass and a clock. It works by computing direction and distance from a known location. After you have learned to navigate with radio nav-aids you may wonder why the FAA spent so much of your time in those awful paperwork plottings of dead reckoning.

Because radios quit, that's why.

Don't ever scoff at dead reckoning or knowing a secondary navigational skill that needs only the reliable old magnetic compass and a watch. Columbus found his way across the Atlantic using dead reckoning. With dead reckoning Lindbergh found Ireland a few centuries later, crossing the Atlantic going the other way.

And he arrived within 5 miles of his intended landfall on the Irish coast.

Dead reckoning, or flying straight toward our destination for the amount of time our speed should take to get us there, would be beautifully simple if it were not for the unseen and ever changing wind drift. Without drift we could just allow for the magnetic compass variation and deviation, then fly a magnetic compass heading straight to where we want to go.

But because a side wind will begin to drift us off this desired *course* line, we need to know something about the direction and force of the wind, and fly "crabbing" into it. How far to turn the nose of the plane upwind is called the *wind correction angle*. Flying along like that, with the airplane not pointed at where you are going, will present a different magnetic compass heading which will be the one you must fly to *track* your desired course line over the ground. The FAA private pilot's course has worked this drift-correcting wind triangle down to an exact science, and you will learn how to make those calculations.

Sooner or later, on one of your student dead reckoning cross-country flights, you will find that your track just happens to coincide with a freeway, a railroad, or a powerline which is going exactly where you are. You will notice while flying enough crab angle to stay over this ground feature and not drift downwind from it that you could have skipped all that wind correction angle paperwork of last night. It's OK. That's part of pilotage, and all of us use such landmarks as a "quickie" way to find drift angle correction, or note known places along the course line that will confirm the fact that we have been flying the correct drift angle. We call these *checkpoints*.

There is a tendency among pilots who are flying along some easy-make ground reference line not to crab into

the wind, but to just droop a wing, or hold a little one-sided rudder and sort of slew along. Don't do it. Turn the whole airplane into the wind enough to correct for the drift, and fly it that way—wings level, straight, and efficiently streamlined as they should be.

After all the pre-flight paperwork of plotting an honest dead reckoning flight, using the radio nav-aids will make you wonder if pilots are not overpaid. The beacons are scattered all over the country, their frequencies, distances, and headings are printed across the charts like freeways, and all you've got to do is tune the beacon properly, stare at the *left-right needle* on the face of the *omni-bearing selector* (OBS), and keep the needle centered as you fly to or from the VOR station that you have tuned in. There is a window in the OBS that reads "to" or "from," and the *left-right needle* will start to drift left or right off center telling you which way to make a gentle course correction if you are drifting right or left off the beam.

The beacon you are flying toward broadcasts a radio signal spoked outward from its center, along each of the 360 degrees of the compass. Each 1-degree spoke is called a *radial.* You tune in the radial that will take you most directly to that beacon, and the left-right needle will tell you if you begin to stray from your course.

These beacons are called very high frequency *omni-directional ranges (VOR)*, often reduced in aviation slang to "omni stations." There are also VOR stations originally developed for military use that have the added feature of distance measuring capability. Called tactical air navigation *(TACAN)*, they are now common to civilian and military use, and a TACAN combined with a VOR is identified on the charts as a *VORTAC.* Training planes are not usually equipped with *distance measuring equipment* (DME). To you and me they are all VOR stations.

The navigation and communication (*nav-com*) radio in your aircraft will be a duplex unit. The com side of it is two-way, with a microphone and a tuning dial to select whatever ground controller frequency you need to use. The nav side receives only VOR stations, with a tuner to select the frequency of whatever beacon you want to use to navigate with.

Both nav and com signals are way up there in the ultra-high frequency (*UHF*) band, and like FM radio

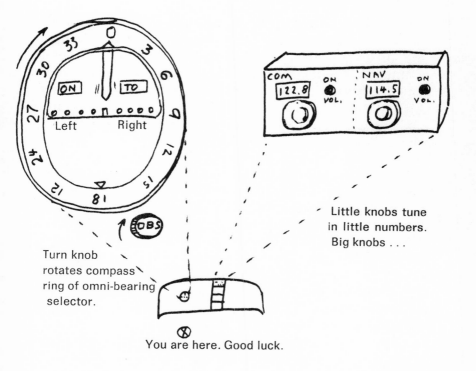

ON || TO

Left   Right

OBS

Turn knob
rotates compass
ring of omni-bearing
selector.

COM
122.8   ON   NAV   ON
        VOL. 114.5 VOL.

Little knobs tune
in little numbers.
Big knobs . . .

You are here. Good luck.

reception, they are clean signals, not much disturbed by
weather or static, but limited to line-of-sight reception.

A rather optimistic table of VOR reception altitudes
is:

    1,000 feet—45 miles
    3,000 feet—80 miles
    5,000 feet—100 miles
    10,000 feet—140 miles

Since nearly everyone navigates between VOR stations, and they are spotted within range of each other
over nearly all the country, the most commonly traveled

straight-line routes between VORs are shown on aeronautical charts and are called *victor airways*, each having its own identifying number, as the freeways do. Printed on the charts, but in considerable clutter of too much information, you can find the frequency of the VOR station, the distance and heading to the next one, and the minimum route altitudes along that victor airway needed to get a clear radio reception and to have a safe ground clearance over any obstacles along the way.

As you can see here, radio nav is a wonderful system, and we all love it and are spoiled by its many good features. The VOR tracks are used by high-flying airliners and low-flying students alike, and they are wonderful when everything is working as it should. We have only touched on the salient features of VOR navigation. I won't spoil the joys in store for you and your future flight instructor when he teaches you how it works and about its subleties and snares.

Long before the VOR system became commonplace, aircraft radio-navigated with *non-directional beacons* (NDB). Non-directional beacons are on the low-frequency wave band, and they pick up static and lightning, fade in and out, and sometimes in the little towns they just quietly go off the air. Nobody notices or seems to care.

If your airplane has an *automatic direction finder* (ADF) radio you can use the non-directional beacons as a backup or supplement to the VORs. Operationally, the ADF radio is simple almost to a fault. Turn it on, tune in the desired frequency, and the fine little needle swings across the face of its compass rose dial and stops, pointed at the NDB station. It says, "It's over yonder."

The disadvantages of the NDB, which probably hastened the invention of VOR stations, are that the needle will just as readily point to a cloud full of lightning as to your desired destination. And static comes

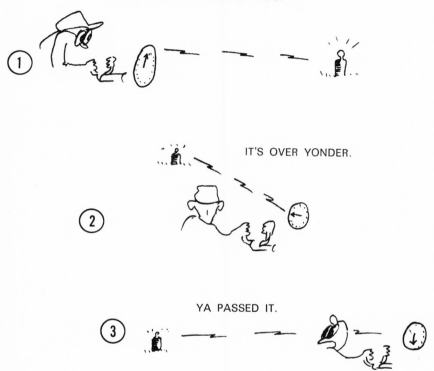

Three simple phases of an ADF needle indicating location
of an NDB beacon

crashing through the audio part of the ADF radio just as
it will on any AM radio station. In fact, you can pick up
the standard AM radio broadcasting stations and listen to
your favorite jock on the ADF. If you know the exact location of his transmitter, sometimes shown on charts, you
can use him for a nav beacon.

There was a young pilot friend of mine who flew
"bank paper"—the rapid overnight delivery of various
checks and other banking instruments, which is a fast-

growing banking service. At one of the remote airstrips on his route the local AM radio station's tower was exactly lined up with the runway, and he used it for a homemade NDB approach. In instrument flying there are many FAA-approved NDB approaches; this was not one of them, but it served his needs. Late on a dreary, rainy night he was letting down through cloud, his ADF needle twitchy but verifying his compass heading and his timing that he was right on the line. When the station began playing "The Star Spangled Banner" he realized with a sinking heart that his nav-aid was about to sign itself off right in the middle of his white-knuckled, low-weather approach. Although the big fans on each side of his cockpit were blowing plenty of fresh cool air, this pilot began to sweat profusely. Urged on by duty and just curiosity to see how this would all turn out, our hero continued his approach. The music ended, but the needle stayed centered. During the time it took for the broadcaster to get up and stroll back and switch off the transmitter, our lad skated out from under the clouds and beheld the bright and beautiful runway lights. He never even told his mother about this. A bold pilot. Young one, of course.

Another problem with the old ADF-NDB navigational system is that it provides no way to sense or correct for wind drift. You are not flying along one straight radial as with the VOR. The needle is only telling you, "It's over yonder." If you only flew the needle, with no dead reckoning to find the drift correction angle, your course would be a long graceful downwind curve. As the wind drifted you away to the right, the needle could only say, "It's over yonder, a little to the left." Not a big correction, but in a long flight your ground track would bag far off to the right, and as you neared the NDB station you might notice that instead of coming in from the south, you were somehow coming in from the south-east.

The ADF is still used as a supplement in IFR flying, but for now most of your radio navigation will be flying VOR along victor airways, those freeways in the sky.

A third transmitter found in all modern trainers is the *transponder*. Not essentially a radio nav-aid, a transponder is nevertheless a vital link in the ground-controller–pilot communication system and can sometimes give you an exact position fix because the transponder allows a radar controller to know exactly where you are at all times. He can see you on his scope. Advanced transponders, and eventually all of them, will also tell the controller what your altitude is.

The transponder is a non-voice transmitter-receiver that sends out a very high frequency (VHF) discrete identifying signal which is received and displayed on a ground controller's radar screen, used mostly at this time for the separation of aircraft through dense traffic areas. The controller can find your plane without your having a transponder, but with one you appear on his screen not just as a blurred blip, but as a brightly lighted signal bearing a numbered code.

When you call approach control at a radar-controlled airport he will assign you a four-digit number which you set to display, one digit in each of the four little windows of your transponder. When he asks you to *squawk ident*, you push the "ident" button on your transponder and both your blip on his radar screen and the amber receiving light on the face of your transponder will glow briefly. That's when you hear from him those sweet words of reassurance, "Radar contact." Your amber light will flash each time his or any other beam sweeps across your aircraft. During a typical VFR flight in a noncongested area when you are not in continuous communication with some ground controller (and there will be such peaceful times), your transponder should be on and set to code 1200. That says to any radar scanner that sweeps your plane and blips your little amber light, "There ain't nobody here but us VFR chickens."

If you are making an approach into a busy airport and they give you a transponder code on initial call-up but you have no transponder or the one you've got is in-op, the correct reply is "Negative transponder." You will almost hear him sigh and mutter about underequipped aircraft bumbling around in overcrowded airspace, and more and more of the metro-centers have pilot notations that non-transponder aircraft may not enter. For now, in order to mix you in with the transponder-equipped planes—in fact, to even find you—he will have to take the time to give you a sharp "radar identification" turn, be sure that the dim blip that made the turn is you, then straighten you out onto course again and bring you on in.

In the dense traffic and rapid-fire radio transmissions around any busy airport, this time and attention is given somewhat grudgingly. Your instruction in flying will include the necessary radio talking technique for you to be able to make clean, clear, and concise radio call-up and position reports.

Most of us try to sound professional on the radio. A complete initial call-up and position report can take as little as twenty seconds, even delivered in a Texas accent:

"Hobby radar, Mooney six-seven-two-seven November."

"Two-seven November, Hobby."

"Two-seven November, reporting Fryed intersection four thousand five hundred feet, have India, landing Hobby."

"Two-seven November squawk 0330."

(Pilot quickly sets this code into his transponder.)

"Hobby, squawking 0330, two-seven November."

"Radar contact."

"Two-seven November."

It would be too lengthy and serve no real purpose to you now to decipher all that jargon. The point is that I rehearsed it first, got it off in twenty seconds, and in that time Hobby Houston radar found me, knew my altitude, type of aircraft, course, speed, destination, and that I had all the current landing information concerning busy Hobby airport. And I knew that he would assist me, not totally protect me, from the traffic swarming around Hobby. The final see-and-be-seen, as always, is still mine. There is another old pilot's saying about too much dependence on radar to navigate for you and keep you clear of all traffic: "Big mother radar can kill you."

Notice too that in the above transmission I always gave my own airplane call letters. In the romantic old days we used to acknowledge by just saying "Roger," which meant we heard and understood. But there got to be too many Rogers in the sky and we·took to running over each other.

Not everybody will enjoy the extra load of learning to broadcast while learning to fly. Mike Shapiro, an old friend of mine, who has been a broadcaster for over thirty-five years, decided late in life to once again pick up his war-taught flying skills. The radio hassle around his homeplate of Dallas was so unnerving to this veteran man of the mike that his instructor flew the plane awhile so that Mike could just practice talking on the radio. Mike finally moved his flying instructions out to the silences of a rural airport, which only postponed the problems but at least presented them one at a time.

If ever you fail to understand the jargon of some high-speed controller, ask him to "say again." If you are still not sure of what he said or even what he is talking about, then for your sake and ours, just tell him, "Two-seven November is a student."

You have every right to be there, he knows it, and nobody wants a plane among us who may not be getting it all clearly. The controller will slow down, speak street English. If he doesn't, ask him to, and say again that you are a student. Same thing if you ever get behind in listening to the report from some whiz-bang weather briefer.

Saying "I'm a student" may numb your pride some, but what the briefer or controller is also hearing you say is "I'm a smart student." What follows is usually a lot of real consideration and special handling. Unlike tyros in any other field of endeavor that I can think of, the aviation student is regarded by the rest of the aviation community with affection and protectiveness. This may be because aviation is still new with most of its growth yet before it and we recognize you as the only new growth; as the continuation. Or, more humanly, it may be that all of us recall our own student flying and first times out within a hallowed memory.

Your first experience with cross-country flying compares to when a kid gets his first bike. For the first time he's out of the neighborhood and on his own in strange traffic. For the first time he'll be making judgments and decisions that will affect his own safety. Your instructor will fly at least three hours of cross-country with you as dual instruction. He will plan the trips to comply with FAA rules so that you will get a taste of all three forms of navigation—pilotage, dead reckoning, and radio-nav. If you have not been into a busy controlled airport, he'll season you at that too.

As you fly the ten hours of cross-country solo, each one will involve a landing at some airport at least 50 miles away from mother and home. Your range will in-crease up to at least 100 miles, and each trip will be enriched by your doing all your own planning and weather briefing. I remember these trips so vividly, as first times are nearly always remembered. The youth of my flying. First times to be alone in the airplane for long periods, not pushing to make every minute count in the landing pattern. Time to lean back and delicately fly the airplane, to get fine-tuned to all of its subtleties, the changing light on its curved contours. To gaze out the window some, too, and enjoy the patterns of the fields, farms, and towns. Oh yes, there was always the nagging thought that I might be getting a little bit lost. Did too, once or twice, but not seriously so. Most of all, navigating my own ship over distances through the air was a satis-faction that has not yet dimmed at all. Not from first times till now.

17

MAYDAY!

Mayday! The international distress call for help. From the French, *m'aidez*, "help me."

A continuing part of your flight training will be how to recognize and deal with in-flight emergencies. Most emergencies come as a surprise. Avoiding surprises is the mark of a careful and thoughtful pilot. The process begins in pre-flight planning on the night before when he collects and surrounds himself with all the information and data that could have anything to do with this flight. It begins with the accumulation of all he can find on winds and weather and how this applies to his own level of skill and the range of the airplane. It's the time for gathering up the needed airways charts and making notations of headings, distances, time, speed, and fuel consumption.

Few private pilots rely on fuel gauges; they start with full tanks or some known amount, and know how many gallons per hour the plane uses at the power setting at which they intend to cruise, and think in such terms as having "five hours of fuel aboard." Notations are made of takeoff time, climb time to cruise altitude, time to switch tanks, and so on. Fuel management also begins in flight planning, although your instructor will be doing it for you in the early hours before you begin cross-country flying.

Weight and balance are a part of planning, for fuel is so much of the useful payload weight of most airplanes. The balance problem will be minimal in the small two-seaters and will get more serious only after you begin to fly long, heavy airplanes that can be overloaded or loaded tail- or nose-heavy. But an understanding of how to read the charts in the owner's manual and compute weight and balance will be a part of ground school training and part of the written exam.

You would be surprised at the number of reported accidents chalked up against professional pilots each year as a result of nonchalance about weight and balance. "Oh, I know this airplane—if you can get it in the door she'll carry it" are the most famous last words.

Would some of you folks like to come sit up in front?
Not overweight—but out of balance

A factory pilot once loaded heavy cargo into the aircraft builder's plane and when he stepped into the aft cabin door the plane tipped back and the tail came to rest on the ground. He walked forward to the cockpit and the plane teetered forward and the nose wheel came down to the ramp again. In spite of a problem as obvious as this he initiated a takeoff attempt. He survived the ensuing crash at the edge of the aircraft factory field and was, we presume, able to walk back and get his little pink slip.

Students spend more time agonizing over the course line of a planned flight than professionals, but this is as it should be. Every element of this student adventure is a new experience. My present practice is to take a translucent yellow marker pen and a straightedge and just draw a line on the chart from where I am to where I'm going. Some pilots just pick up the map by these points and crease it. Others follow the jigs and jogs of the published airways between VOR stations more carefully. Either way, the yellow marker overlay is a helpful guide for quick in-flight glimpses at the chart.

All of us should make notations of the radio frequencies we anticipate using enroute. This is because VOR frequencies and approach and tower frequencies are often buried in chart clutter and are hard to read on a bouncy day when you are busy and need them most.

I also make notations of the last weather reports I could pick up before departure, and write down the winds-aloft figures.

All this notation of frequencies, headings, hours of fuel, switching-tanks time, weather, and subsequent in-flight computing of drift angles and ground speed obviously calls for one more piece of paper. There are mail-order specialty houses that make a good living supplying various inventions for doing this cockpit flight planning and accounting. There are devices which clip to the yoke, lap boards, and various knee pads, all sold with the suggestion that the airline pilots use them. In truth, the airline pilot probably has the stewardess on his knee or is figuring his time sheet.

My experience has winnowed all this down to the need for what I call "The Piece of Paper." That's what it is. And the best one I can find is the government printed form that has all the stuff on one side that you call in to the FSS when you open your *flight plan*. It's called "The Flight Plan." Gummed booklets of them abound even at little airports. I use the backside of the flight plan for all this other bookkeeping, then save the flight plan for filling out my log book later, and for whatever claims I can make to the tax people at IRS still later after that. Some of these old, sweat-stained and crumpled pieces of paper become quite dear, recalling as they do all the key events of that particular flight.

And although there is no rule that says that you must file a VFR flight plan with the FSS, the act of doing so can also become quite dear to you. In the unlikely event that you do not arrive at your planned destination within a reasonable time of your estimated time of arrival (ETA), the FSS will become concerned and start looking for you. First by telephone, up and down the route you planned to fly, to see who talked to you last by radio. Then, if inquiry at your destination airport or homeplate reveals that they, too, are looking for you, a search by air is launched. A search much simplified by having on file your flight plan, including your type and color of aircraft, planned route of flight, hours of fuel, and "souls on board." (I've always been intrigued by the FAA use of the term "souls on board" rather than "how many people in plane." I recently learned that the FAA does have at least one good reason for listing the occupants of an aircraft as souls. There is a thriving flying hearse business in general aviation. Small private planes are used to bring bodies back home because, as one such operator put it, "people persist in dying in the wrong places." You can see the confusion that would result if the FAA flight plan listed persons on board, and a flying hearse were to be involved in a fatal crash, and the investigators found one of the persons to be already embalmed.) A filed flight plan is your assurance that if you should vanish into the blue the volunteer Civil Air Patrol air search organization will go into motion, seeking the destination of that particular airplane and its souls on board.

Only a little imagination is needed to guess how these friends will feel if they find you home, safe in bed, having only forgotten to close your flight plan with the FAA upon arrival.

All IFR flights are on a flight plan, and that is one of the reasons why the system works, but a VFR pilot can still wander off into the freedom of whatever uncontrolled airspace there is left, without having spoken a word to anybody. The filing of a VFR flight plan is optional, but it is free insurance.

It is highly likely that you will enjoy a lifetime of flying and never experience an engine failure, but emergency landing procedures will be taught to you before you solo. The instructor will reduce power to idle, tell you that you've just lost the engine, and actually let you glide down toward whatever forced-landing field you have picked out.

Before there were reliable air-cooled engines, the old barnstormers did not count the day complete without at least one forced landing. Of course their old biplanes landed slow, and had big tires which were designed more for pastures than airports, and there was more

open countryside then. But in the back of their minds
the old-timers were always ready, always had some field
in sight they could safely land on. This is the trait we
want to carry over to you. Let it be a comforting
thought, not morbid, to have a "plan two."

A good forced landing is exactly like a normal landing. Even if the engine quits on takeoff, allow yourself
only gentle turns and a normal glide angle. Snug the
harness tight and don't panic. The odds are very high
that you will walk away from this. Aim it at something
cheap that looks as if it may have some give to it. A
wooden shed is better than a brick wall. Then plan to
just land it going straight ahead, wings level, slow as
you can go.

For years pilots have walked away from such 40-knot
crashes. The ones who didn't were those who tried to
turn back to the airport. Entering into a steep turn while
gliding low and slow will take you right out of the gene
pool.

If, during your simulated emergency landings, your
instructor wants you to go below 400 feet with the
power still off, this might be one of those few times to
override him. Just apply the power, pull up, and tell him
that all the best books say not to go that low.

Another really good forced-landing hint comes from
Duane Cole, who says never to glide away from the field
you have selected as a forced-landing site. You will be
flying away from the field if you use a rectangular landing pattern. You risk extending the downwind leg farther than you can glide back on final. Duane's common-
sense solution is to glide down over the field in a shallow
turning circle. You will always be looking at your intended touchdown point from this circling-buzzard,
overhead approach.

Nothing as serious as practicing for a forced landing

can escape the gallows humor of the other face of flying. In this spirit, I pass along to you advice I got on what to do if the engine quits on a night cross-country flight: Set up a normal glide, wings level, and carefully descend to an altitude of 50 feet. At 50 feet, switch on the landing light. If you do not like what you see, switch it off.

The radio can be a great help and comfort during an emergency. For one thing, it's important to have someone know you are going down, and even better if you can tell them where.

For many reasons, pilots are reluctant to declare an emergency. There seems to be some misinformed lore that declaring an emergency will go onto your "record" or cause some long hassle with the FAA. Not so. I have declared emergency twice. Once to get an immediate IFR clearance during a sudden encounter with fog, and once to report slowly failing engine power. In the first instance the immediate reply from my call of Mayday brought an immediate answer from a nearby FSS station at a time when I had not been able to raise anyone. He gave me frequencies to use for clearance, I got them, and that ended the matter.

When I lost power, I was north of Mobile, Alabama, and again got an immediate answer from Mobile approach. They got a radar fix on me, gave me vectors and distance to the field, and no, there were not any small, uncharted airstrips on the way. Mobile gave me immediate landing clearance. With sputtering engine we made it to the airport and landed. On the ground the engine ran strongly, and the tower wryly suggested I check for carburetor ice. All they wanted after that was my home address over the phone from a very red-faced pilot. Hell, I didn't know that a carburetor would ice up in level cruise on a clear cool day; I thought it could only happen if I reduced power. And anyway, my

Mooney never had carb ice before or since.

The moral of this story is twofold: It is smart to call for help if you think you need it even if it turns out to be embarrassing later. Also, never assume that something is not the cause of the trouble just because you have never had it happen before.

FAA controllers are skilled and prompt in handling Mayday calls, and think of it as a part of their profession. Most of their calls come from low-time VFR pilots lost or trapped above overcasts.

If you do not get just a little bit lost at least once during your student days you will be a most rare fledgling. Here are my dos and don'ts on being lost. Understand, I have never been lost. There have been some long, anxious intervals when I was not exactly sure where I was—but I was never lost.

One would not say that Lindbergh was lost when he sighted the first fishing boat off the coast and swooped down and yelled from the *Spirit of St. Louis*, "Which way is Ireland?" He knew that he was over the Atlantic Ocean, knew that Ireland was somewhere on the other side, beyond the big E on his compass. He may have just been lonesome to talk to somebody, or get local street directions. Whatever, the Irish fisherman just stared at him, and he went on and flew E to Ireland.

The don'ts for being lost are: Don't fly in a circle and don't fly off on some "hunch." The dos are: Fly one straight compass heading, follow a railroad or a freeway if you can because they always lead to something—and radio for help pretty soon.

Lost on a student cross-country trip, I followed a railroad to a nice little town, hoping to find its name on the water tank as a nav-aid. I really don't think the old-fashioned water tank will ever be totally replaced by VOR, NDB, and all that electronic wizardry.

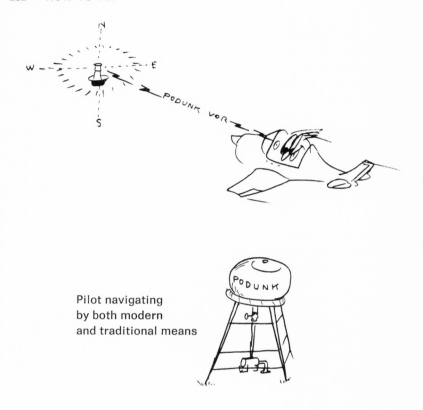

Pilot navigating
by both modern
and traditional means

Unfortunately, this town had no name on the water tank, so I quietly glided the little Aeronca down by the school bus parking lot. They nearly always have the name of the town painted in big black letters on school buses. Not here, not with this tightwad board of trustees. Either that, or I was over School Bus, Texas.

One other uncertain time I flew a good freeway to a nice-sized town, could see from a distance the bold lettering on the water tank, made an apologetic low pass by the thing only to find it lettered, "Seniors—'58." I put a curse on that whole class and flew on down the freeway looking for a town with a more civilized water tank.

The absolute guaranteed way to find your position is to land at the next airport you see and buy a little gas. The logic behind buying a little gas is: You can never have too much gas anyway, and you can avoid the everlasting memory of being the guy who taxied up to the ramp and got out and said, "What town is this, anyway?" Few airports are civil enough to have the name of their town painted somewhere prominently. You buy the gas, get a receipt, and find the address on the FBO's gas ticket. Don't be too anxious and grab at it and start looking at it right away with big sighs. They will be on to you right away. Be casual, pocket the ticket, and saunter around the corner to the restroom and there in privacy you can relieve both your mind and body. One of the salient rules of flying, never found in other instructional literature, is: "Never miss a chance to pee." Or to buy gas. You don't really ever have to admit later that you have joined the large fraternity of pilots who, if not lost, have suffered temporary lapses of knowing exactly where we were.

When signaling an emergency in flight, for being lost or for any other reason, we have three means available. In a descending order of how well they work these are:

Just pick up the mike and say "Mayday" on the frequency you last had good communications on. Or switch to 121.5, which is the always-guarded emergency frequency that should never be used for any other reason except being in trouble.

Or set your transponder at 7700 and squawk ident. A special code flashes out. The controller who sees it may not know what your troubles are, but he will at least know exactly where you are, and that's a comfort. You may flash 7600 because you have lost two-way radio communication in a controlled airspace. After squawking emergency 7700, switch to 7600 and squawk that. This is the code saying that you have lost radio communications. The controller will begin to experiment with you to see how much radio you have left. "If you can hear me, but can't transmit, squawk ident again." Then he will know that you can hear him but cannot reply and a sort of binary language link will have been established.

Or if you are in a radar environment, start flying large triangles, 2 miles to the side. If only the transmitter is inoperative, make right-hand turns. If both transmitter and receiver are out, fly left-turning triangles. There may be some pilot who has been noticed doing this, but I have yet to find him. What is supposed to happen is that they will send out a plane to guide you in.

If you ever have to make an approach to an airport which has a control tower and you have no radio, just aim at the tower, fly by it rocking your wings, then get into the landing pattern, spaced as nicely as you can if there is other traffic, and land. The first words from the line boy will be, "Tower wants you to call them on the phone." You do that promptly, and explain that you were experiencing a no-radio emergency. And that's what it had better be, too.

To summarize aircraft emergencies: They are seldom an instant event that requires split-second reactions such as those typical of highway travel. For the most part you have ample warning of a pending mechanical problem. If the engine runs rough during the mag check on preflight, don't go. In flight, aircraft engines seldom just quit cold. I have never had it happen. But I have seen warnings from the temperature or pressure gauges, felt the engine roughen up in flight, and there was always time to land at the nearest airport. Those events, over a quarter century of enjoying flying, could be numbered on one hand. The absolute best time to troubleshoot an ailing engine is when standing on the ground beside a mechanic, not in flight with the hair standing up on your neck.

The majority of "Mayday!" experiences in general aviation involve some slowly culminating mechanical problem, or some wrong decision made by the pilot. Weather and fuel management still lead the list of in-flight emergencies, and the pilot knows very well that he is tempting fate by flying into marginal VFR weather when the most simple emergency action would be not to take off, or if already airborne, to make that wonderful old 180-degree turn and get the hell out of there. And a pilot knows very well that he is creating a possible emergency situation when he overflies an airport where he could make a fuel stop, but continues onward with get-home-itus and his fuel tanks mostly filled with air.

It is obvious that you personally will have the most control over in-flight emergencies by the prior mind-set you have taken toward flying. David B. Noland, one of the editors of the valuable but controversial *Aviation Consumer* magazine, said it well: "It's up to each pilot to weigh the risks and benefits. . . . After all, risk management is what the art and science of flying is all about."

And from the United Kingdom's National Safety Council: "No one gets ready for an emergency in a moment. What a person does in an emergency is determined by what he had been doing regularly for a long time."

I went to three experienced airline pilots, asking if they had any sage words on this subject. Two of them were aviation-struck kids, working as line boys, when I was a private pilot renting airplanes from the Feuge brothers, FBOs at Orange County Airport at nearby Orange, Texas. Both of the pilots now fly Delta airliners off cement airports for a living and little airplanes off grass airports for love. I asked them all this question: "If you were talking to a person just learning to fly, what advice would you give them?"

Their answers were surprisingly alike.

Mike Trahan said, "Don't hurry anything. In over twenty years of flying I have never had to hurry."

Larry Pullan said it a little more obliquely: "In an emergency, first wind your watch." What he meant was, take the time to think it out and take some deliberate action rather than make some hasty reaction.

The third airline pilot was Floyd Addison, who had started when they were Delta Dusters, flying old bi-planes out of Monroe, Louisiana, and stayed with Delta through all its history up to modern jets. At the time of our visit Floyd was nearing sixty and retirement. I asked him if he felt the slowdown of reaction time of an older person might affect his capacity as captain of a DC-8 jetliner. I am old enough myself to be able to ask a man a question like that.

During our visit in my home I had been secretly fascinated with Addison's mannerisms as he sat in an easy chair which had broad, flat wooden arms. We had been exchanging books, serving coffee, and a number of small items had accumulated on the chair arms. I have never seen a man whose movements were so unconsciously careful and deliberate. It was as if we had recreated the cramped office of a DC-3 flight deck and all the other switch-and-lever-crammed pilot's spaces that he had spent his lifetime in. The old captain never made a sudden or broad gesture. In my imagination I could see him picking up the check list and going through the procedures with his co-pilot with an engine-out alarm shrilling in his ear, just as it must have happened many times in his lifetime of flying.

Captain Addison's reply to my question about lightning-fast reactions was obvious in everything about him, even before he said, "Most times it's better to pause a few seconds and make sure you have correctly identified the problem and that the action you are about to take is the correct one."

The best advice I could get for you from the three airline pilots amounted to the same thing: Whether you are making your pre-flight walk-around, or going down the cockpit check list, or responding to some in-flight emergency, it is best not to hurry.

And also don't be too proud to ask for help. There was a local private pilot here a few years ago whose last words on approach control's tape were the brave, restrained, and professional-sounding, "Ah, I seem to be having a little problem here . . ." Then he went vertigo and into the East Texas piny woods wilderness on a dark rainy night. Calling "Mayday" might have alerted someone to the seriousness of his "little problem"—might have gotten him the help that he needed, which can sometimes come with just the reassuring sound of another human voice over the radio.

18

FREE AT LAST

Throughout this book we have looked ahead to the time after you solo, or when you begin to fly cross-country, and the forty hours of flying time and the written exam you must pass to get your private pilot's license. Now let's take the lid off that box and examine its contents in an orderly fashion. Let me lead you like Hannibal's elephants onto the peak of the Alps to see how far we must climb and how steep the path before we go back and pick up the load.

One of the joys of learning to fly is that it will be hands-on experience for you from the first encounter. One of the surprises of flying is how soon you will solo. Although still a student in the eyes of God, man, and the FAA, you really are a pilot flying an airplane the first time you do it alone.

It's traditional not even to hint to the student that he is about ready to solo, although that's mostly what instructors gossip about among themselves. "Yeah, he's about ready. One more hour of landings like he was doing last time and I'm going to cut him loose. . . ."

Nowhere in the FARs does it specify the number of hours before solo. The bottom line in FAR part 61.87 simply reads: ". . . by an authorized flight instructor who finds that he is competent to make a safe solo flight in that aircraft."

Under General Requirements, Flight Proficiency Training, the requirements are:

(i) Flight preparation procedures;

(ii) Ground maneuvering and runups;

(iii) Straight and level flight, climbs, turns and descents;

(iv) Flight at minimum controllable airspeeds, and stall recognition and recovery;

(v) Normal takeoffs and landings;

(vi) Airport traffic patterns, including collision avoidance precautions and wake turbulence; and

(vii) Emergencies, including elementary emergency landings.

The solo flight must be made within ninety days of the last dual instruction entry in your logbook. But I hope you don't wait that long. You'll do better the day after your last dual.

The instruction you get before they turn you loose in the airplane is really bare-bones basic. You'll only know how to start it up, take off, circle the field without hitting anything or stalling out, and do a landing you can walk away from. And that's all they will ask you to do on solo. The rest of it is so easy to learn that it will soon become obvious that what the person beside you in those first few unforgettable hours is looking for is a safe approach and a smoothly controlled landing.

Gannaway used to say of my early approaches and high-bounce landings, "Baxter, your recovery from odd attitudes at low altitudes is excellent. However, sir, if this does not get better soon I may give up flight instruction as hazardous to my health and take a mail-order course in taxidermy."

And all of that was in the old Aeronca, which was a tame and forgiving airplane. Later, when circumstances made both Gannaway and the Aeronca no longer available and I had to switch over to Brown Airport, Orange, Texas, and Vanneman and the Luscombe, Van did not load up my mind by telling me that Luscombe was going to be a more sudden handful of airplane to land. I found out soon enough.

All of these airplanes were "taildraggers," and if touched down not aligned with the runway, or allowed to start swerving during roll-out, the heavy end, which was the back end, wanted to get around in front. This is called a *ground loop.* Damage is mostly to the pilot's pride and dignity, as the airplane—wings tipped, tires screeching—makes sudden looping circles along the runway.

All taildraggers tend to ground-loop if not managed carefully. It will not be a problem in a modern tricycle-gear trainer where the heavy end is in front and the dynamics are such that the rolling plane seeks a straight line forward.

After ground-looping George Mitchell's old Stearman biplane I came into the pilots' ready room for coffee and to face the grinning, sun-bronzed ag pilots there who had heard it all and knew exactly what had gone on out there on the turf strip.

"Mitchell," I asked this careful and safety-conscious ag operations owner, "what is the best thing to do about a ground loop?" You can cover some stupidity by asking scholarly-sounding questions.

"I'm glad you asked that, Bax." And all his pilots grew silent and serious, listening. "If the Stearman is allowed about 10 degrees off angle from a straight-ahead landing roll it will try to go around on you. Proper use of rudder and some moderate braking after slowing down will keep the landing straight ahead as it should be. However, there is one thing you can do once a ground loop is fully developed and you hear the tail going by you and you are getting a swift 360-degree view of this airstrip. . . ."

"What's that, sir?"

"You fling both hands high into the air, and in a loud clear voice you yell, 'Aw-ww, shit!' "

Roars of laughter, pounding of coffee cups on the table.

With Van in the narrow-legged, stiff-kneed Luscombe, I was having directional control problems on the ground. Van cured a lot of this by just telling me I was "ground-shy." He had me race up and down the airport, controlling the airplane with my feet. Later, I worked out my way of getting used to seeing ground-related objects whisking by at low altitudes and approach speed. I just went out and flew down the long, smooth, deserted beach, sometimes even nursing the plane down low enough to roll the wheels lightly in the hard sand. I got used to how things looked, and the perspective of peripheral vision which is such a help in landing. A better and more legal way of doing this would be to simply ask the tower for a low pass down the active runway until you get used to these sensations and cure yourself of "ground-shyness."

Perhaps because of my years (I was middle-aged when I learned to fly), perhaps because I flew old planes and had to switch from one to another, I was late approaching the solo hour. But one day, after a string of good landings, Van said, "Slow it down to a full stop out here. I think I got a cramp in my foot and I want to get out a moment."

This coyness, this not letting the student know until

the last moment, may reduce a lot of anxieties. But I said to Vanneman, "If you are getting out of this airplane for the reason I think you are, sir, you got a cramp in your head."

We both knew that I was about ready. Van took out a white handkerchief, said he would use it to signal me to go on around and do more landings. "Now just take it around the pattern by yourself."

There are few rites of passage in the human experience as memorable as your first solo flight.

The plane seemed lighter, rose up and flew sooner. It also seemed louder, and I was more aware of all the rattles, whines, and wind-moans of the old Luscombe. Turning downwind I could see Van, a tiny figure down there in the middle of the airport, all alone. (Your solo is also an important event for your instructor. He has made a serious career judgment.)

It seemed funny to think that was Van down there on the runway; the phantom of his bulk seemed to be still beside me in the cockpit. I could hear his voice, and sometimes still do, calling out approach speeds, when to turn, saying to keep her lined up straight with the runway.

And there was a feeling of some kind of glory. There is no doubt in your mind that you have sprung the surly bounds of earth. That you are flying. A pilot.

Oh, not yet, not really. You still have most of the hours of instruction ahead of you, and the exam, too. But in this little informal drama at the airport you have been turned loose in an airplane for the first time.

This solo flight was about all the pioneers ever got. If they soloed, they were pilots and flew away to learn the rest of it as best they could. The licensing of planes and pilots dates back only to the mid-1930s. Solo is all that Lindbergh got, and he finished learning to fly carrying passengers for pay. Carrying passengers for any reason is strictly forbidden to student pilots today. Any person beside you must be a licensed pilot.

But there I was, as pilots say, flying a plane alone. Alone at last. Scared? Not at all. Excited? Yes, plenty.

Time now to settle down and concentrate on a good landing. Everything felt good coming in on approach, looked just right. No, too high! Oops, too late. There she goes, settled right out from under me. *Wham!* Down and stayed down. Where is Van? Ah, there he is beside the runway, waving that white handkerchief. What for? Surrender or go around again? I applied takeoff power.

A good takeoff, but more jittery about the landing this time. High again, drifting off to one side, wing down, gonna lose it! *Ker-wham! Wham!* Down on one leg of that stiff landing gear. Boy, what a hard airplane! Snatch it, catch it, she's getting away swerving left, wheels plowing up turf, ground-looping off the runway.

Mr. Edgar Brown, the fine gentleman who owned the airport, had planted sorghum corn in the wide places between the runways. Good airport land utilization. I was headed for the tall corn.

Brakes! It tipped up. Off the brakes and into the slender sorghum corn. It made a sound like running a stick along a picket fence. Fodder blew all over the windshield, the tail tipped up again, and we settled down. We stopped. Sorghum corn is a very good airplane absorber.

Van. Oh, how I hate to see Van. I'm sitting there, prop ticking over. Leave it running, this looks like a bad place to try to hand-prop a plane to start it. Van is coming through the newly cleared swath, head down, hands in pockets, kicking a clod now and then.

He ducks under the wing, peers at me scrunched up in my hole. I peer back. "Well, we can't leave it like this, can we?" said Van.

Van gets ahold of the outer wing strut, I gun the engine some, we get it heaved around, pointed back out. Van steps back, sweating, nods to me. I get back out on the runway and take off again.

Now for one really good landing to make up for that excursion into the fodder. Flying the pattern cools me, confidence returns. Coming in nicely—and just as I'm ready to call it a landing, it all goes to hell again. Too slow, too high, the wing droops again, stalling and falling those last few feet, coming in skewed at the grass blades once more. I know what it's going to do.

Ker-whump! Wham! Screee . . . Same damn thing. Well, nosir, not if I can help it. Stick and rudder hard over, body English too, I ride it all the way around in a tight circle, but gain control and straighten it out still on the runway and let it coast meekly up to where Van is standing, pretending he was not ready to run.

He ducked under the wing, opened the door. Our eyes met. "I guess we better call it a day," said Van.

"Yessir."

"Your landings are a little slow and high, but your taxiing I could sell tickets for." We laugh, he gets in—elbow to elbow, the brassy smell of our sweat. Comrades, we taxi carefully back to the hangar.

Bad as it was, I was elated. I could hardly stand still as Van wrote the solo endorsement in my log book. Some of the hangar japes were there, enjoying. They saw it all; no need to talk about it as we stood beside the hot, sorghum-smeared, gray Luscombe.

Suddenly Van cried out, "I guess we better cool you off, you hot pilot!"

Pilot! He had called me pilot! I had not recognized that Vanneman's chunkiness was heavy muscle. He picked me up, yelling and kicking, carried me lightly on one hip to the airplane washing stand and hosed me down good. I drove home wet from the airport that day, making up loud songs and singing them at the top of my voice. Pilot. He had called me a hot pilot.

I never fly over Orange County Airport, as it is now called, without looking down there and seeing the faded, phantom-gray Luscombe edging low around the pattern, me alone and free inside it, still hearing Van's voice from the empty right seat.

The Luscombe, N71246, must be still flying somewhere. Old Luscombes never die. But I never got to fly her again. Last heard of, Alfred Grant Vanneman was flying four-engined transports. All of this was about a quarter century ago. I hope your solo will not be as eventful as mine, but I'll bet you the memory of it will be as vivid twenty-five years later in your own life.

There is still some kind of a horseplay ceremony to mark the end of your first solo flight. Hosing down and symbolic horse-trough dunking may have gone out of style, but when you suspect you are getting close to becoming a "pilot," start wearing an old shirt you can spare. The current tradition is to catch you, cut off the shirttail, and print your name and date of the event on it in bold black marker pen. In the little airports they hang rows of these trophies along the walls of the pilots' ready room.

After solo you can settle down and seriously go to work on the forty hours, which is divided into twenty hours of dual instruction and twenty hours of solo flying. In the twenty hours of dual time you will fly three hours cross-country and three hours at night. In the twenty hours of solo flying, ten of it will be on cross-country flights. The twenty hours dual does not precede the twenty hours solo in a solid block of flying time. After you solo, and ever afterward, dual instruction is intermingled with solo flying as needed.

The FAA has placed some good common-sense restrictions on the flying privileges of the student pilot. You may not fly solo unless your log book has been endorsed by a flight instructor who has flown with you within the last ninety days. This dampens the dangerous and irregular practice of a student's taking dual only up to solo, or maybe a few hours more, and then just flying off and forgetting about the rest of it as they did in days of yore. A lot of those brave yores never lived very far into the yon.

The other most important student restriction is that you may not carry passengers. This means that Mom will just have to wait to ride with you until you have your private pilot's license—unless, of course, she already has hers.

Passing your private pilot's written exam and flight test is nothing compared to the emotional impact of first solo. The written and flying tests are separate, and may take place at different times and places. Flying will be much the same for you as for a licensed pilot except that you may now bring the family, while remaining "clear of clouds."

The primary restriction against a private pilot is that he may not carry passengers or cargo for hire. Again the FAA has allowed some decent exceptions to this rule. You may accept money in compensation for a flight in connection with a business if the flight is only incidental to the nature of that business employment. Yes, you can charge it to the company if you are calling on the trade at 110 mph through the air instead of at 55 mph down the road. A private pilot may also accept money as shared operational expenses with passengers. At 200 hours you will be eligible for an instrument rating, and again I seriously urge that you set this as your next goal. A brand-new IFR rating does not make you a "weather pilot," ready to go busting out of the jaws of some midnight sleet. That kind of stuff scares most of us. But being an instrument pilot enables you to utilize fully all of the equipment in a modern aircraft and to fly with the full benefit of the "system" and all the aids of today's Air Traffic Control Centers.

Most of my instrument time has been accumulated in small increments: taking off into an overcast, or descending through it in an orderly fashion at my destination. All the flying in between has most often been in bright hours of sunlight on top of low, silvered cloud layers.

At 250 hours total flying time you are experienced enough to take the commercial pilot training and exam. In addition to licensing you to fly for hire, this rating refines your flying skill some, and deepens your knowledge of the FARs. It is one of the least demanding tests within the upgrading of your license.

Most demanding, after the instrument rating, is the *air transport pilot* (ATP). An ATP candidate must be at least twenty-three years old, be "of good moral character," and have 1,500 hours total time as a pilot. A friend of mine, the president of a large aviation corporation, decided to gain his ATP on the home-study course and enjoy full privileges with the professional pilots who fly his company's transport-category aircraft. After six months of study he presented himself to the examiners. Asked how it went, he replied, "Well, at least I got my name and home address right." The exam was structured around a hypothetical flight of a Boeing 707, New York to Rome, with him as pilot in command and responsible for coping with fuel flow, transocean meteorology, international regulations and law, and what would be the weight and balance configuration of that aircraft on final approach in Rome. The ATP rating, held by transport pilots, is the Ph.D. of aviation. It is not uncommon for the applicant to fail the test on his first try.

One of the main reasons for the astonishingly good safety records of airline travel and corporate biz-jet flying is the rigid regulatory structure that both planes and pilots must exist within. Private pilots and light planes are not much less protected, but with less than an ATP rating and a lifetime good-paying career on the line, private pilots are more lax, more casual, and seem to say, "That's a good ruling, but doesn't really apply to me."

One might think that just saving your hide in an airplane would be incentive enough to fly sanely, but over 75 percent of the general-aviation crashes include at least one violated FAR on the way down.

Look at our record:

Although the FARs require us to be taught the recognition of hazardous weather, and any student should be able to safely get home under a legal VFR minimum ceiling of 1,000 feet, the greatest single accident cause is still "VFR pilot continued into IFR weather," breaking the rules and his branch of the family tree.

Another major cause of accidents is fuel exhaustion. But how could you run out of gas if you flight-planned with the thirty-minute reserve for day VFR, and forty-five-minute fuel reserve for night VFR and all IFR, as required by the FAA rules?

So many drunk pilots are carried out to the cemetery by fellow aviators that a wake joke has grown up around the applicable FAR: "Oh, was it eight hours from the bottle to the throttle? He thought it was eight feet."

The FAA examined you very thoroughly before granting that pilot's license. Under strict FARs, your commercially licensed training plane was inspected at every one hundred hours, and your privately owned plane gets the same inspection once a year. In truth, an airplane gets a fresh airworthiness inspection every time a pilot does a walk-around pre-flight of it.

As a licensed pilot you come in for inspection once every two years. Dual inspections, actually: one before a flight surgeon, who will sign his name and certificate number only if you are physically fit to fly; the other by a flight instructor, who will ride with you and then endorse your log book only if you can still perform all the things your license says you can.

The net result of all this is that flying is much safer than it used to be, and the proof lies within the stony hearts of those who figure up life insurance actuary tables. In the 1930s, pilots shopped long, and paid dearly, for life insurance. Most were simply refused. In the immediate postwar period when I began to fly, our old family insurance company added a one-page "rider" with an "aviation clause." After 600 hours, their odds showed that I was now the same risk as any other car and driver and the extra flying cost was waived.

A cursory check with contemporary insurance betting odds on pilots reveals that it's a courtesy to advise your local agent that you have been smitten with flying, but the general practice is to not modify an existing policy. If a new policy is written as your student days begin, expect extra costs only for the first hundred hours. After that, those who are putting money on how long you will live will not raise the odds just because you are now a pilot.

Your own decision to fly by the FARs will eliminate 75 percent of the risk in aviation, but you will be sorely tried. The first test may come on that first long student cross-country flight.

Summer clouds have begun their afternoon buildup, and aviation weather is reporting scattered thunderstorms along your pathway back home. You are at some strange, distant airport, trying to find someone who will talk to you about weather. Your instructor is back home in the operations shack, pacing. Cursing.

Bob Walker, veteran CFII and FBO at Beaumont, says it succinctly: "That's my ticket he's flying on. . . . Not really, but I signed him off to go fly."

If you should call him collect from out there and tell him you don't like the looks of it and that you are going to sit it out awhile, you may hear his long breath of relief, but you'll never know if he had tears in his eyes.

The First Rule has yet to be revoked: There are old pilots, and there are bold pilots, but there are no old bold pilots.

In my own early and unforgettable days of student cross-country flying, Vanneman did something that made him dear to me forever. Coming back from Galveston on the dual cross-country, with me uptight as spider claws about course keeping and getting lost, he made a great stir of settling himself into the back seat of the Aeronca, clasped his hands over his chest, and after a few loud yawns, pretended to sleep the rest of the way home.

Then when I flew the same trip first solo, he handed me a small blue card with a hole cut in the middle of it. "This is your blue card instrument ticket. With this not even you can get in trouble. Before you start back, hold this blue card up against the sky. Look through the hole. If the sky is not the same color as the card, don't go."

Is flying an art, a science, or a skill? There are opposed views within the two faces of flying. In truth, the best of it combines all three.

There is also folklore in flying, and I give you now the

essence of it. The three most useless things in an airplane are:

1. Runway behind you.
2. Altitude above you.
3. Fuel tanks carrying air.

But the soundest and most poignant words written
into the library of flying came unintended as philosophy
from the legal minds of the FAA. It is found in the FARs'
paragraph 61.43 (6), and has to do with the stringent
qualifications of flight tests. It is a truth that lives:

"(6) Showing that he is the master of the aircraft,
with the successful outcome of a procedure or maneuver
never seriously in doubt."

Some of the very best and most beautiful hours of my
life have been spent in little airplanes. Someone once
asked how much money it took to get into private flying,
and I answered, "All of it." Any good folly is worth
whatever you are willing to pay for it.

And flying seems to call out the poet that lies within
men's souls. You find it in Ernie Gann's *Fate Is the
Hunter*, and every page of Saint-Exupéry's *Night Flight*
and *Wind, Sand and Stars* is pure free verse. Flying
completed the transfiguration of Richard Bach from pilot
to poet to mystic. It's not uncommon. Harry Stinson
said, "Flyers have brought themselves out to the edges
of the unknown spiritual world."

Commander V. M. Voge, M.C., writing in the Naval
Safety Center's *Approach* magazine for August 1980,
removed some of the veil of mysticism from all this.
After a careful and analytical study of all these raptures
that pilots kept coming back with, Voge dubbed the
experiences as the "Breakoff Phenomenon": "The Breakoff Phenomenon usually occurs only at rather high alti-

tudes (30,000 feet or higher). It is often described as a weird feeling of detachment, isolation, remoteness, and separation from the earth and from the aircraft. One feels he has broken the physical bonds of earth, or as if he is being balanced on a knife edge. Occasionally, the aviator may feel that he is outside his own aircraft and body, watching himself fly. . . ."

Commander Voge goes on to describe the manifestation as most likely to occur on long solitary flights, constant heading, poor horizon, and lack of customary visual cues of external motion. He points out, and I must agree, that the Breakoff Phenomenon is not limited to high-altitude jocks, but has been experienced by helicopter pilots flying as low as 500 feet over the seascape on a hazy day.

I have had a few truly extraordinary moments even as I was parked right on the ramp. I had always wanted to be an airline captain, admired them, knew I was never good enough to try, even as a youth. But shortly after buying my first airplane, I was parked at the transient ramp at Houston Intercontinental Airport. It ought to be called the "tramp ramp." It's the bone tossed to little airplanes that might need to beg in among the big jets at the terminal to pick up or deliver a passenger. It was a hot day, and I had my cabin door open and was sitting in the sun on the wing of my little Mooney waiting to pick up a business associate. The ramp tug brought in a huge B-727 and carefully moored it to the gate next to mine. A few feet farther back and I would have been sitting in the shade of his wing. As it was, my Mooney squatted there barely as high as the airliner's front tire. After a while the commotion and stir died down around my tall neighbor, and high above me, way up past the bulging sides, a window clicked open and slid back, and a crewman studied me from his lofty right seat. Air conditioning lightly ruffled the feathers under his uniform cap as the youthful flight officer leaned out and gazed down upon me and my flying machine as if he were peering down from the bridge of the *Queen Mary* at some dockside flotsam that had drifted up alongside. We gazed at each other, me craning up into the sun.

At last I called up to him, "You the co-pilot on that thing?"

He nodded, a fleeting smile stretching his fine-clipped mustache.

"Well," I called up to him, "I'm the captain on this one."

Softly he withdrew his head and clicked the window shut. Right then I would not have taken a million dollars for my little twelve-year-old airplane, or the pilot's license to fly it that was in my pocket.

GLOSSARY

active runway The runway being used by aircraft taking off and landing.

ADF See **automatic direction finder.**

adverse yaw An unwanted opposite turning effect caused by the difference in drag and lift of the aileron positions during a turn.

aerobatics or **airbatics** The spectacular and sometimes violent maneuvering of an aircraft, usually associated with air shows. The Federal Aviation Authority rules that occupants wear parachutes in a bank of over 60 degrees or a climb or dive of over 30 degrees.

aeronautical charts Designed especially for flying, two major categories are those with ground features clearly shown for VFR (Visual Flight Rules) flying, and those in which radio beacons and routes are emphasized for IFR (Instrument Flight Rules).

Aeronca Pioneer light aircraft first made by the Aeronautical Corporation of America, 1928. Affectionately called "airknocker."

ag flying The planting, fertilizing, and insect control of crops by aircraft.

AGL Measurement of altitude from above ground level.

agonic line A wavy line following the earth's magnetic field from the North Pole, over the Great Lakes, Appalachian Mountains, and into the sea off the Atlantic coast of Florida. Along the agonic line there is no variation between geographic north and magnetic north.

ag pilot Short for agricultural pilot; a refinement of "crop duster."

ailerons French for "little wing." Hinged control surfaces on the wing, the opposed movements of which control the roll axis of the airplane.

airfoil Cross-section shape of the wing; a long teardrop shape.

Airforce One An airplane assigned to the President of the United States.

airframe The structure of an airplane, exclusive of engine, instruments, and radios.

airline transport pilot (ATP) The highest pilot certificate issued by the FAA. Applicant must be 23 years old, and have at least 1500 hours total flying time, along with other requirements.

airport traffic area A controlled airspace 5 miles in diameter, and upwards to, but not including, 3,000 feet above the surface.

airspeed The forward speed of an airplane, fast enough to create lift and support the plane in flight.

airspeed indicator A flight instrument with a calibrated dial, readout of which is called "indicated airspeed."

airstrip An airport with only one runway.

Air Traffic Control Center (ATCC) The enroute part of the FAA ground control system, managing traffic out along the airways.

Air Traffic Controller (ATC) An FAA employee who directs traffic by two-way radio, as from the control tower at an airport.

airworthy Describes an airplane that meets all the regulations and a pilot's inspection and is ready to fly.

altimeter A flight instrument with a calibrated dial which reads the altitude of the airplane above a given level.

angle of attack The angle between the wing chord line and the flight path of the airplane.

angle of incidence Built into the airplane, a small up-angle between the wing chord line and the centerline of the airplane.

approach That part of a flight in which the airplane draws near the airport. Also slang for approach control.

approach control An FAA ground controller who by two-way radio, and sometimes assisted by radar, manages the flow of approaching and departing aircraft, usually within a radius of about 20 miles from the airport.

approach pattern The designated directions and altitudes flown around an airport while descending to land.

artificial horizon A gyro-driven flight instrument with a moving graphic display which depicts the attitude of the aircraft in flight as related to the horizon line.

ATC See **Air Traffic Controller.**

ATCC See **Air Traffic Control Center.**

ATIS Airport Terminal Information Service; the continuous broadcasting of wind, weather, altimeter setting, and any other pertinent information to a pilot approaching an airport. Usually found only at medium to larger airports, readable at about a 20-mile range.

ATP See **airline transport pilot.**

attitude The attitude of an airplane as related to the level horizon of the earth. Diving would be a nose down attitude.

attitude indicator Another name for **artificial horizon.**

automatic direction finder (ADF) A low-frequency radio navigation system with an indicator needle which points to the magnetic compass direction of an NDB (non-directional beacon). When used as a part of the radio array of an instrument landing system, the beacon is called an LOM (locater, outer marker).

autopilot A complex device, usually found only on larger and more sophisticated aircraft, which the pilot can set to control the attitude and direction of flight without his hands on the controls.

avionics A catch-all word to describe the radios and radio navigational systems of an airplane.

bank To tip the airplane out of level flight along its roll axis.

barnstormer Slang for the gypsy pilot who lived out of his airplane and hip pocket during the 1920s and 1930s when the airplane was still only a novel attraction.

base leg One of four sides to the landing pattern; it crosses the downwind edge of the airport from downwind leg to final approach turn.

Beechcraft Airplanes built by Beech Aircraft Corporation, named for Walter Beech, who founded the company in the mid-1920s at Wichita, Kansas. Beechcraft are still made there. They have always been high-quality airplanes that cost more, fly faster, and last longer.

biplane An airplane with upper and lower wings. The Wrights flew a biplane, a design concept that dominated aviation for thirty years before giving way to faster, more efficient monoplanes. Biplanes are still built for fun and aerobatic flying.

blind flying Obsolete slang for instrument flying.

booster pump An auxiliary fuel pump, usually used as safety backup to the regular, engine-driven fuel pump during takeoff and landing.

"Break right" To make a sudden right turn. One of several terse directions that may be given by an airport controller to separate collision-course traffic.

B-727 Described by Braniff Captain Len Morgan in his *Boeing 727 Scrapbook* as the "DC-3 of the jet age," this three-engined, short-to-medium-range 105-passenger jet transport was introduced in 1964 and to date (with over 1,500 in service) is the most widely used transport plane in history.

bush pilots Slang for the irregular and daring pilots who pioneered air service in undeveloped countries. Mostly associated with Alaska—an association that modern Alaskan scheduled flying is attempting to overcome.

buzzing Low flying, steep turns, showing off over beaches or the girlfriend's house. Also called "flat hatting" by the Navy, and reckless flying by the FAA. Dangerous and illegal.

cage To use the "caging knob" on a gyro flight instrument to restrain its movement. Usually one cages in resetting the instrument.

cam A pear-shaped lobe on a rotating shaft to produce reciprocating movement in some machine part perpendicular to the shaft.

camber The arched upper surface of a wing.

carburetor heat The carburetor heat knob on the control panel diverts hot exhaust gases into a jacket around the carburetor to warm the carburetor throat and prevent the formation of carburetor ice.

cardinal altitudes In VFR flight, altitudes established to separate traffic by having westbound traffic—magnetic heading 180 degrees to 359 degrees—fly at even altitudes plus 500 feet. Eastbound traffic flies at odd altitudes, zero to 179 degrees, plus 500. IFR traffic uses the same compass divisions, but flies at odd or even thousands.

CDI See **course deviation indicator.**

ceiling The height above ground of the lowest layer of cloud cover.

center Common slang for Air Traffic Control Center where FAA ground controllers manage enroute air traffic.

Certified Flight Instructor (CFI) Person who is certified by the FAA to teach student pilots to fly.

Certified Flight Instructor, Instrument (CFII) A flight instructor who is additionally certified to teach instrument flying. Often called a "CF double I."

Cessna 150 First model of an all-metal, two-place, high-winged, 100-hp training plane.

Cessna 152 Second model with 110-hp, and minor refinements. Most popular training plane of the '70s and '80s.

Cessna 172 Four-seat, 160-hp version of same family of planes.

Cessna 182 Four-seat, 230-hp, still-bigger model of the largest-selling family of airplanes in the world.

Champ Nickname of the Aeronca Champion—prewar/postwar forerunner of the Citabria. Same basic airframe.

check list A prepared list of pre-takeoff and post-landing procedures, sometimes on a permanent card in the cockpit, sometimes on a placard on the instrument panel . . . and sometimes missing.

checkpoint A recognizable ground feature or object by which a pilot can verify his own location while navigating.

check ride A flight test ride in which the instructor or examiner flies with the applicant to observe his skill level.

chocks Metal or wooden wedges or blocks, placed around the wheels of a parked airplane to prevent the plane from moving.

chord The width of the wing, measured at its widest point from leading edge to trailing edge.

Citabria A late-model Aeronca Champion, built and powered for airbatics. "Airbatic" backward.

"Clear" The warning word shouted out the window by the pilot before engine start-up.

clearance Written or verbal permission from an FAA controller; e.g., "Mooney 27 November is cleared to land."

cockpit Old-fashioned word dating from World War I, but still used to denote cabin or flight-deck area occupied by pilot.

commercial ticket A license to fly cargo or passengers for hire, issued by the FAA after a detailed examination requiring more experience and knowledge than the examination for the private pilot license.

commuter A short-haul airline flying between populous areas. Breeding ground for future airline pilots.

compass rose An old seafaring term, carried over into aviation, to describe the face of a compass. Often printed on charts as an aid to flight planning. Usual configuration is north at the top, with large index marks every 30 degrees between east, south, west, and north.

constant speed propeller See **controllable pitch propeller.**

continental control area All airspace above 14,500 feet above mean sea level.

controllable pitch propeller Gives the pilot control of the pitch angle of his propeller blades, could be compared to a "low gear" for climb power and a "high gear" for faster, level cruise. Technically correct term is **constant speed, controllable pitch propeller.** Either usage OK.

controlled airport One with a control tower, equipped with two-way-radio traffic management.

controlled airspace Areas requiring two-way radio clearances from FAA controllers, such as Airport Control Areas, Terminal Control Areas, and restricted areas, as shown on charts, and all airspace above 14,500 feet, the floor of the Continental Control Area.

control surface Rudder, elevators, ailerons—those hinged, movable surfaces which control the airplane about its four axes in flight.

control tower The tall structure at the airport, filled with government employees who, visually and with two-way radio and radar, direct the traffic on and about a controlled airport.

control wheel As often called the yoke, the control which replaced the "stick" for moving the ailerons and elevators.

control zone A controlled airspace of 5 miles or more around one or more airports, extending upward to a specified limit. Control zones are sometimes irregular in shape, as shown on charts, to accommodate instrument-flight approach and departure paths.

Convair Properly the Convair Division of General Dynamics Corp., makers of military and aerospace hardware, but intended here to describe a 40-passenger, twin-piston-engined airliner which picked up where the DC-3 left off in short-haul routes in the 1950s and 1960s. Convairs, stout airplanes, are still used by some commuter airlines.

convection currents Rising columns of unevenly heated air from the earth. Buzzards and gliders love them, low-altitude cross-country pilots bump along through them.

coordinated flight When the aircraft is flown true to its streamlined, designed axis, not slewing or skidding to the outside of turns, nor slipping to the inside of turns because of the skilled coordinating of the pilot's touch at the controls.

co-pilot A licensed pilot who can perform all the functions of flying the aircraft, but is subject to supervision of the pilot in command.

Corsair Also known as the "Bent-Wing Bird," "Angel of Okinawa," "Whistling Death." Famed U.S. Navy-Marine fighter plane that entered the Pacific war in 1944. Designed by Chance-Vaught. 2,000 hp, 395 mph. Popularized in the TV series *Baa Baa Black Sheep*, which was based on the true-life book of Major "Pappy" Boyington, who, with 26 victories, was the top Marine ace.

course also **course line** The direction or heading of an airplane in flight.

course deviation indicator (CDI) The more commonly called "left-right" needle on the face of the OBS (omni-bearing selector), an instrument whose face presents a visual image of flying the VOR radio navigation beacon system.

cowling The sheet-metal covering of the engine and engine accessories; part of the nose of an airplane.

cross-controlled Opposite from coordinated flight; a time when, for example, left rudder is applied to right-turning aileron forces.

cross-country In common usage, a cross-country flight is one of any distance in which you land at a different airport. A local flight is one in which you take off and land from the same airport.

crosswind A surface wind that is blowing at an angle across the active runway.

crosswind leg One of the four sides of a landing pattern; it crosses the upwind edge of the airport between upwind leg and downwind leg.

cruising altitude A general term meaning the altitude you have selected to level off and cruise at. In instrument flight it is the granting of a clearance for the pilot to select his own cardinal altitude anywhere below 18,000 feet.

Cub The affectionate and proper name for the most famous of all the pioneer two-place light planes. The Cub, now called Super Cub, has been in production at Piper Aircraft since the early 1930s.

cylinder head temperature gauge An engine instrument which measures the temperature of the most critical and hottest spot of a running engine.

DC-6 A four-engined, piston-powered transport plane of the immediate postwar period, built by Douglas Aircraft.

DC-9 A twin-jet, medium-size transport plane built by MacDonald-Douglas, still very popular in medium-length and national flights.

dead reckoning A method of navigation having its origins in ships and ancient sea travel. The navigator finds the direction with a compass, allows for drift, and times his progress with his known speed against the distance.

dead stick Old time aviation slang, still very much in use, to describe a glide or landing without engine power.

de-icing Sophisticated devices to prevent the formation of ice on aircraft in flight.

density altitude The measurement of altitude as influenced and changed by the addition of heat, which tends to "thin" the air, giving it the effect of a still-higher altitude.

designee As in "FAA designee," a person qualified by the FAA to hold certain positions, such as examiner for the FAA.

deviation The error in a magnetic compass caused by its proximity to metal and electrical devices built into an aircraft.

dew point When the temperature of the air reaches the dew point, water vapor appears as fog, dew, or frost.

directional gyro Also called the heading indicator. A gyro-driven flight instrument that takes its setting from the magnetic compass, and thereafter acts as a steadier, easier-to-read compass itself. Called a "compass repeater" on ships.

distance measuring equipment (DME) Usually found only on more sophisticated aircraft, the DME not only tells the pilot his heading to the VOR beacon but also his distance, and some give a readout of ground speed.

dive An airplane diving toward the earth is at a steeper angle of descent and flying faster than gliding.

downwind leg One of the four sides of the landing pattern; it lies parallel to the active runway, but it is flown downwind in the opposite direction.

drag The wind resistance to the total frontal area of an airplane in flight. One of the four forces of flight. Thrust must be greater than drag to increase speed.

drift A sideward movement away from the desired course line, caused by the movement of the air ocean through which the airplane is flying.

drift correction angle The degree of nosing upwind enough to compensate for the downwind drift and thus to follow a true track along the desired heading.

dual controls Duplicate yoke and rudder pedals so that either of two occupants can fly the airplane.

dual instruction The time that a student or pilot flies with an instructor present in the plane.

dusting Slang term for **ag flying.** Not favored by the ag aviation industry today.

elevator The hinged control surface at the rear of the horizontal stabilizer which controls the pitch axis of the airplane when the yoke is moved forward and backward.

enroute control The use of radio or radar by FAA air traffic control centers to space aircraft safely apart by distance and altitude along cross-country flights. Always a part of IFR flights, the service is optional to VFR flights through uncontrolled airspace.

Ercoupe A light, two-place airplane with metal fuselage and fabric-covered wings. A bubble canopy covers the cockpit. Small twin rudders are linked to the aileron controls in such a way that rudder pedal controls can be omitted. One of the first light planes to use a tricycle landing gear. Designed by Fred Weick in the immediate postwar period, the Ercoupe was too advanced for its time. Ercoupes persist and are liked, although attempts to manufacture and sell them have failed repeatedly.

FAA examiner Field representative of the Federal Aviation Authority.

FBO See **fixed base operator.**

Federal Air Regulations (FARs) The written rules and regulations having to do with aircraft, their manufacturing and operation, and the people associated with aviation such as pilots, mechanics and controllers.

Federal Aviation Authority (FAA) The governing body of civil aviation under the Department of Transportation.

ferry A non-revenue flight to move an airplane from where it is to where it ought to be.

fin The vertical part of the tail assembly to which the rudder is hinged on its trailing edge.

final approach The last part of an airplane's maneuvering through the landing pattern, when it is lined up with and descending to land upon the active runway.

fishtailing A seldom-seen maneuver, used by the old biplanes on final approach. The rudder is sawed from side to side, causing the airplane to slow down and descend, while giving the pilot a good forward view past his engine.

fixed base operator (FBO) Person operating the "airplane store" at the airport, dealing in sales, service, renting, and instruction of general aircraft, and in student training.

fixed pitch propeller One in which the blades are not adjustable.

flame-out Slang term used by jet pilots to describe an engine failure.

flaps Hinged control surfaces at the trailing edge of the wing, inboard of the ailerons. Flaps move downward together, allowing the pilot to decrease his stalling speed and thus land slower.

flare-out The delicate leveling-out of the landing airplane at the end of its final approach. As airspeed decays, the nose is lifted slightly, and the airplane is said to flare out and land.

flight controller An FAA ground controller trained at his duties as either tower operator, enroute controller (ATCC), or Flight Service Station (FSS) person.

flight deck The area occupied by the pilot and other flight crew. Associated with airliners and aircraft requiring more than one crew member. They still call it the cockpit, too.

flight instruments Those instruments grouped before the pilot which guide him in the attitude and directional control of the aircraft.

flight line A general term for the ramp or area in front of the hangars or FBO's office where aircraft are lined up and parked.

flight plan A description of your airplane and its intended flight, usually submitted to an FAA facility before the flight. A requirement in IFR flying, optional but recommended in VFR flight.

flight service station (FSS) Located at larger airports, an FAA facility open to pilots for personal visit or by in-flight radio if enroute. The FSS is not involved in traffic control, does give traffic advisories, weather briefing, and other flight condition information. Many of these friendly desk-front manned centers are being replaced by automation.

flying speed Enough airspeed over the airfoil of the wing to create lift and flight.

forced landing An unscheduled landing, usually caused by mechanical problems or weather avoidance.

fuel selector A manual valve in the fuel system, located in the cockpit to allow the pilot to select which fuel tank to operate from. Usually combined with fuel supply on-off valve.

fuselage The body of an airplane. From the French word *fuselé*, "spindle-shaped."

general aviation That part of the aviation community not engaged in scheduled airline or military flying.

glide A gentle power-off descent.

G-loads Term used to describe the increased gravity load on an airplane caused by centrifugal force during maneuvering. "A tight, two-G turn" would double the weight of the aircraft.

go-round A balked landing. Power is applied before touch-down and the airplane goes around the pattern again.

gross weight All that an airplane is certified to lift when it is loaded full of people, cargo, and fuel.

ground control That part of the operation of a controlled airport where the FAA ground controller in the tower visually directs ground movements of aircraft and vehicles on the surface of the airport.

ground effect A compression of the air flowing between the wing and ground when the airplane is about one wing-span above ground. Creates additional lift, is most noticeable in low-winged aircraft.

ground loop A wild but usually harmless out-of-control maneuver, happening mostly to taildragger airplanes, when the tail, or heavy end, gets ahead of the nose while landing.

ground school That part of a formal student training pro-gram in which the FAA written exam is prepared for in a classroom.

ground speed How fast the airplane is tracking over the ground. The only true measure of how fast an airplane is flying.

Grumman also **Grumman American** Large aerospace military manufacturer that acquired the American Aviation Corporation in the early 1970s and began to build the Grumman-American line of light aircraft. At this writ-ing the manufacturing of Grumman light aircraft has ceased.

gust locks Simple mechanical devices placed on the con-trols.or control surfaces of parked aircraft to prevent their swinging and banging in the wind.

gyro Short for gyroscope. A rapidly spinning small wheel mounted to be free in its movement about one or more axes of spin. The gyro offers considerable resistance to any forces that would move it from its own spin axis, and therefore can hold a constant horizontal or vertical plane. Although the aircraft it is mounted in may be banking or turning at random, the gyro can display a constant horizon or steady direction.

hangar A building designed to house aircraft.

heading indicator Another name for the directional gyro, which is set from the magnetic compass and then repeats the compass heading but in a steadier and easier-to-read manner.

high As used to describe aviation weather, an area of high barometric pressure usually associated with clear skies.

Hobbs meter A small meter usually grouped on the right of the panel with engine instruments. The Hobbs meter displays in hours and tenths of hours the total time that the engine has been running.

hood time A casual term to describe the hours that a student spends wearing a hood which restricts his view to only the instrument panel. Used with an instructor during simulated instrument flight. The plastic hood is small and lightweight, like a cardsharp's visor, only more so.

horizontal fin Same as horizontal stabilizer.

horizontal stabilizer The wing part of the tail assembly to which the elevators are hinged.

hypoxia Oxygen starvation, the condition of the occupant of an aircraft who has been at too high an altitude for too long without enough oxygen. First symptoms are euphoria; last ones are unconsciousness and death.

ident Term used in operation of the transponder. When the ground controller asks the pilot to ident, the pilot pushes the so-marked button and his blip on the controller's radar screen glows brightly for instant identification.

Instrument Flight Rules (IFR) Apply when the ceiling is below 1,000 feet and visibility is less than 1 mile.

instrument panel That part of the airplane forward of the controls, below the windshield, upon which the instruments are mounted.

instrument pilot One who can fly in IFR conditions. To get such a rating a pilot must have 200 hours total time, 40 of which must be simulated, or instrument-instruction, flying.

isogonic lines Shown on most charts as broken red lines, the isogonic lines depict the eastern and western variations of magnetic north from geographic north.

Jenny The Curtiss JN-4. Standard training biplane of World War I. Thousands of new ones were sold cheaply as surplus. These two-seaters were the cussed and beloved favorites of barnstormers up into the mid-1930s.

joystick Obsolete slang for the control stick of the early airplanes.

knots A nautical term for indicating speed per hour. Used in instrument flying and becoming more common as a standard in VFR flying. A knot is 1 nautical mile, or 6,080.20 feet, per hour. Don't say "knots per hour"; it's like saying "miles per hour per hour."

Kollsman window The small opening in the face of an altimeter through which the pilot can read the barometric pressure number when he has set his altimeter to correspond with that pressure. Named for its inventor, Paul Kollsman, and first flight-tested by Jimmy Doolittle when the General was an Army test pilot experimenting with instrument flight in 1928.

land To descend from flight and alight on earth in a controlled manner . . . or nearly controlled.

landing gear The wheels and their connecting struts that an airplane lands on and uses for ground travel.

landing light At least one very bright spotlight that a pilot can switch on to illuminate his point of landing at night.

leading edge The forward edge of an airfoil, strut, or fin.

lean To reduce the amount of fuel in the fuel-air mixture at higher altitudes where less fuel is required in the thinner air.

Lear Jet From the genius of Bill Lear, a pioneer personal-business jet aircraft—small and very fast. Introduced in the early 1960s.

left-right needle See **course deviation indicator.**

lift One of the four forces of flight. When lift overcomes gravity an airplane can fly. Lift develops over the wings when an airplane reaches its flying speed.

line boy An employee of the FBO who tends to the parking and fueling needs of aircraft on the flight line. Some of these boys are girls.

liquid compass Another name for the magnetic compass.

locater out marker (LOM) The non-directional beacon (NDB) that is a part of an instrument landing system, only a few miles out from the threshold.

low As used in aviation weather, an area of low barometric pressure, usually associated with bad flying weather.

Luscombe Airplane designed by Don Luscombe. Most commonly seen are the rugged aerobatic two-seaters with metal fuselage and fabric wings. These clean high-winged monoplanes were popular in the immediate postwar period. Long out of production, but long-lived. Nearly every country airport has a Luscombe somewhere.

mag check A part of the pre-flight; one turns the ignition switch from "Both" magnetoes to "Right," then "Left," watching for a drop of over 100 RPM, which would indicate ignition troubles.

magnetic compass The old-fashioned simple compass with an indicator floating in alcohol, one end magnetized to point to the magnetic north pole.

magneto An electrical generator using permanent magnets to generate current for ignition.

main wheels The pair of wheels that are built for the landing load, as opposed to the nose wheel or tail wheel.

master switch Turns off all the electrical systems in an airplane except the ignition.

Mayday The international distress call for ships and aircraft. From the French *m'aidez*, "help me."

mean sea level (MSL) Altitude measurement from sea level as opposed to altitude above ground level.

mixture control The engine control knob that leans out the fuel mixture to get less fuel at high altitudes where there is less oxygen.

monoplane An aircraft with a single wing.

Mooney Fast fuel-efficient and strongly built all-metal four-place monoplane. Designed by Al and Art Mooney. Their Kerrville, Texas, firm foundered, was bought as a subsidiary to Republic Steel, and thrives today. Aging Al lives in a house trailer near Kerrville.

multi-engine An aircraft with more than one engine. Requires a pilot with a multi-engine rating.

mushing Pilot slang for flying too slow to maintain level flight or climb, but too fast to stall. The plane "mushes along."

nautical mile A term more associated with navigation at sea; used for instrument flying, and growing in use for VFR flying. A nautical mile is 6,080.20 feet, as compared to a statute mile of 5,280 feet.

nav-com Abbreviated slang for navigational and communications two-way radio in aircraft.

needle and ball Pilot slang for the rate-of-turn indicator, or turn-and-bank indicator. So called because the visual display features a needle and ball.

non-directional beacons (NDB) The older, low-frequency radio navigational beacons first used in radio navigation and still in use to supplement VORs.

non-precision approach An instrument approach that does not use a glide-slope beacon to determine the proper rate of descent.

nose wheel The third wheel, under the nose of the airplane, not intended to absorb hard landing loads.

OAT Outside air temperature.

oil pressure gauge A part of the engine instrument cluster that gives the pilot an instant readout of the all-important oil pressure.

oil temperature gauge A part of the engine instrument cluster that gives the pilot the temperature of the engine oil system.

omni Short for omni-directional indicator, or a display confirming the receiving of the signal from a tuned-in omni or VOR station. Omni and VOR are interchangeable phrases for the same thing. The display appears on the OBS head.

omni-bearing selector (OBS) A rotating ring around the face of the visual display of the VOR receiving equipment. With a station tuned in, rotate the OBS ring until the needle centers and the compass rose on the OBS ring gives you the heading to or from that station.

partial panel To fly the airplane with part of the flight instruments covered up by the instructor, simulating a failure of some of the equipment.

P-factor Propeller factor. The left-swerving tendency of an airplane on takeoff, and left-yawing in full power climb, caused mostly by the spiral prop wash passing back along the fuselage and pushing against the rudder and fin from one side.

pilotage The oldest and simplest form of navigation, a matter of looking out the window and knowing where you are from recognizing features on the ground.

pilot in command (PIC) Means exactly what it says.

Piper One of three major aircraft builders in the U.S. Company founded by Bill Piper in the early 1930s, and thriving today with a complete line of aircraft from the Cub on up through the modern two-place trainer—the Tomahawk—and into a range of turbo-powered, medium-sized fast twins.

pitch The nose-up, nose-down pitch axis of a plane in flight.

pitot Pronounced "pee-tow." Named for French physicist-engineer Henri Pitot (1695–1771), who developed the principles of this static tube collector to measure the flow of fluid or gases. It is an L-shaped fixture, opening to the front, beneath a wing leading edge, and furnishing variable air pressures through the pitot-static vent system of the aircraft to operate such instruments as the airspeed indicator, vertical speed indicator, and altimeter.

power setting Pilot's expression to indicate the amount of horsepower being used, such as 100 percent on takeoff, 75 percent in level cruise.

practice area A non-controlled bit of airspace near the airport but far from airways routes and climb or descent corridors where an instructor and student may go work together in peace and safety.

precession The word to describe the creeping error built into a directional gyro that requires it to be periodically reset to the magnetic compass.

pre-flight The inspection of an airplane by its crew before flight to be sure it is airworthy. A regular ritual using the check list.

prime To feed fuel to the engine before starting. Some engines are primed by pumping the throttle rod, others by a separate prime pump. Either injects raw fuel into the cylinders for easier starting.

private pilot One licensed to fly by the FAA but not to carry passengers or cargo for hire.

propeller The airscrew that delivers the power of the engine into the forward thrust of flight. Major parts are blades and hub.

prop wash or **prop blast** The spiral thrust of air moving back from the propeller when it is in motion.

radial In radio navigation, this means one magnetic compass bearing from the hub of the VOR beacon, such as "the 180-degree radial," meaning exactly south of the beacon.

radio deck or **radio stack** The area, usually in the center of the instrument panel, where the nav-com radios are mounted.

rag doll Slang term of affection for an old fabric-covered airplane.

ramp Another name for the flight line, or paved area for parking and maneuvering on the ground in front of the FBO offices or hangars.

rate-of-climb indicator See **vertical speed indicator.**

reciprocal heading The opposite direction. The reciprocal heading of 180 degrees would be 360 degrees; the reciprocal heading of 30 degrees would be 210 degrees.

relative wind Created by the motion of the airplane in flight.

In an airplane the relative wind blows over the nose in the same direction as the flight path.

retractable landing gear One of the characteristics of a complex airplane which can retract or tuck up its wheels in flight for less drag and better speed.

rich In describing the fuel-to-air mixture, rich means more fuel than the engine needs.

roll See **slow roll.**

roll axis One of the four axes about which an airplane is free to move in flight. The ailerons control the roll axis —raising one wing, lowering the other, causing the airplane to roll, or bank along its centerline.

roll-out The expending of energy after the touchdown of landing.

RPM Revolutions per minute. The scale of measuring how fast the engine is running.

rudder The movable control surface hinged to the rear of the fin which controls the yaw axis, one of the four axes of flight movement.

rudder pedals The foot pedals rising from the cockpit floor that allow the pilot to swing the rudder left or right.

rudder trim A fine-setting control, not usually found on light trainers, that can add a small amount of yaw into the rudder.

running rough A common term to describe an engine that is not running smoothly.

run-up To increase the power setting of the engine while the airplane is parked prior to takeoff for the purpose of pre-flight testing of various engine functions.

run-up area A broad place in the taxiway, usually at the end where it turns to the runway, provided for the pre-flight run-up of the engine at a distance from the ramp to isolate the noise and prop blast.

short-field takeoff To perform one, the pilot sets the brakes, runs up full power, starts rolling, lifts the nose wheel as soon as possible, lifts the mains as soon thereafter, but remains just off the surface in ground effect until safer flying speed is attained before climb-out.

shutdown The process of turning it all off at the end of a flight. Turn off all avionics, set the engine at full lean until it stops, then switch off ignition and master switch. Use check list.

sideslip See **slip.**

sink Pilot's expression for the descent of an airplane mushing along in slow flight, too slow to maintain altitude.

skid A cross-controlled uncoordinated turn. The airplane skids to the outside radius of the turn.

slip The opposite of a skid. The airplane slips to the inside of the turn.

slipstream The flow of air along the surfaces of a plane in flight.

slow flying Maintaining flight with as little power and airspeed as possible, while either going straight ahead, turning, or attempting to climb.

slow roll An airbatic maneuver in which the airplane is slowly rolled all the way over along its longitudinal axis like a chicken on a barbecue spit.

snap roll An "automatic" maneuver. An abrupt and violent horizontal spin that an airplane can be forced into by slowing it down, nose high, and jamming the rudder all the way to one side while yanking the stick all the way back into that same side corner. A very steep turn, usually past 60 degrees, will set up a cross-controlled situation to sometimes make an airplane "snap" unintentionally.

soft-field takeoff Same procedure as a short-field takeoff.

solo Only the pilot in the airplane.

span The measurement of the wings from tip to tip.

spin An "automatic" maneuver similar to a snap roll, only with the airplane pointed downward instead of horizontal. Can be induced by prolonged holding of cross-controls while the plane is in a deep stall.

"Squawk ident" What the ground controller usually says when he wants you to push the ident button.

stabilator A made-up word to describe a one-piece horizontal tail plane which does not have separate stabilizer elevator.

stabilizer See **horizontal stabilizer.**

stall, stalling speed A stall is a condition in which the airplane's wing is held at too high an angle of attack for too long. The slipstream burbles, then separates from the airfoil and the wing can no longer lift. Stalling speed is as slow as an airplane can fly straight and level.

static system vent A dime-sized fixture, usually back on the fuselage in a low pressure area. Vents the input from the pitot tube.

statute mile The standard land mile, 5,280 feet.

Stearman Actually a Boeing M-75, called PT-13 by the military, but affectionately known as the Stearman, for Lloyd Stearman, its designer. Ten thousand of these rugged two-cockpit biplanes were built for Army and Navy use as primary trainers during World War II, making them the "Jenny" of that postwar period. Thousands were sold cheaply as surplus, converted mostly for use as ag aircraft. Today the Stearman is the prize of collectors, restorers, fun flyers.

stick Same as joystick.

struts The wings of a biplane are held in place by wing struts. The landing gear of an airplane extends from the fuselage to the wheels on landing gear struts. The wings of a Cessna monoplane are braced by a single diagonal strut fixed between outer wing and lower fuselage.

student pilot An aviation trainee who has a student pilot certificate and is working toward getting his private pilot's certificate.

supercooling The harmful and rapid cooling of an airplane engine that is reduced to idle power during a prolonged glide from cool, high altitudes to landing.

surface winds The winds blowing across the surface of the ground, usually at a different speed and direction from winds aloft.

TACAN Tactical Air Navigation. A VOR station with distance-measuring capability, primarily designed for military use, but usable by general aviation traffic as well.

tachometer An engine instrument which reads out the revolutions per minute (RPM) of the engine.

tail assembly The rudder, fin, horizontal stabilizer and elevators. The tail feathers of a plane.

taildragger Slang for an airplane with a tail wheel instead of a nose wheel.

tail surfaces Same as **tail assembly.**

takeoff The speed-gaining run of an airplane down the runway to achieve flight.

taxi, taxiing The movement of an airplane on the ground, excluding takeoff or landing.

Taylorcraft or **T-Craft** Light two-place, high-winged, fabric-covered monoplane. Forerunner of the Cub, later rival of the Cub. Designed and built by G. C. Taylor. Still in production at this writing, at the original factory.

TBO Time before overhaul. The number of hours that the manufacturer recommends an engine may run before it is rebuilt.

terminal control area (TCA) Most often called the TCA and in slang "the birthday cake," because its diagram on charts looks like a tiered birthday cake upside down. Found only at the busiest airports. Entering the TCA may require at least a private pilot certificate and a transponder in addition to two-way radio. Size and shapes vary to meet local traffic needs.

threshold The approach end of the active runway.

throttle The engine control that opens the carburetor to a greater or lesser amount of fuel. Determines at what power setting the engine will run.

thrust One of the four forces of flight. The power of the engine, delivered through the propeller, develops thrust. When thrust overcomes drag the airplane moves forward.

torque The tendency of a running engine to produce a rotational force about its crankshaft axis.

touch-and-go A description of landing practice in which the pilot completes his approach, flares, touches down, then applies power and goes around for another.

track In navigation, the actual pathway of the airplane over the ground.

traffic pattern The orderly flow of landing aircraft around an airport, as prescribed by that airport's management or the FAA control tower.

trailing edge The back edge of a wing, rudder, or any such part of the airframe.

training plane Usually a light two-seater of simple, strong design and construction.

transponder A non-voice transmitter-receiver that sends out a very high frequency, discrete identifying signal which is received and displayed on a ground controller's radar screen as a means of locating and following that aircraft through dense traffic areas.

trim tabs Smaller control surface, set into the trailing edge of the primary control surfaces, operated by the trim wheel to give a minor and constant "trimming" of the airplane to achieve zero or neutral pressure on the controls, or make minor changes in flight attitude.

true north The geographic north pole of the earth.

T-tail An aircraft with its horizontal tail plane mounted on top of the vertical tail plane.

turbine More commonly called "jet engine."

turboprop A jet, or turbine engine, that delivers its primary thrust through a geared propeller.

turn-and-bank indicator What it says. Often called the "needle and ball," which describes its appearance.

turn-and-slip indicator The same as above.

UHF Ultra-high frequency radio.

uncontrolled airport An airport with no operating control tower.

uncontrolled airspace Those places left in the sky where it is not necessary to be in two-way radio communication with any FAA ground controllers.

uncoordinated flight When the aircraft is allowed to slip or skid in turns, or skew along in level flight because of the deliberate or unintentional uncoordinated uses of the controls by the pilot.

UNICOM The frequency set aside for communications at an uncontrolled airport. Predominantly 122.8 at this time.

unscheduled landing More polite term for a forced landing.

upwind leg A part of the landing pattern when the pilot is flying parallel to the active runway and into the wind.

variation In navigation, the degree of difference between true north and magnetic north.

vectors Flight directions given to a pilot by FAA ground controllers.

vertical speed indicator (VSI) Also called rate-of-climb indicator, a flight instrument that does not measure altitude, but instantly and accurately does measure change of altitude and displays this rate of change in feet per minute.

VHF Very high frequency radio band, such as a VOR station.

victor airways Like freeways in the sky. The most commonly flown cross-country routes between navigational radio beacons. Numbered and plainly shown on aeronautical charts.

Visual Flight Rules (VFR) To be used flying clear of clouds.

VOR Very high frequency omnidirectional range. VOR stations are also called omni stations. The most commonly used beacons in air navigation.

VORTAC A VOR station combined with a TACAN which gives both direction and distance from the station to aircraft equipped with DME (distance measuring equipment).

wake turbulence See **wing tip vortices.** Spiral vortices that trail outward and downward from the wing tips of an aircraft in flight. The wake of large heavy aircraft can upset and damage light planes.

walk-around Casual term for the pre-flight inspection in which the pilot walks around the outside of the airplane, inspecting it in a prescribed and routine manner. Done before each flight.

weight and balance Catchall term to describe the limits, loading procedures, and regulations that are followed to ensure that an airplane is not loaded beyond its certified gross weight carrying capacity, nor carrying its load dangerously too far forward or aft, which would affect its balance.

wet compass Common slang term for the magnetic compass.

whifferdill Slang term to describe a wild—planned or unplanned—maneuver in flight.

whiskey compass Macho slang for the magnetic compass.

wind correction angle The angle at which an airplane is headed upwind to offset the amount of downwind drift and be able to track a true ground course to the destination.

windsock Common term for the pole-mounted, fabric tube at the airport. Its large end is free to swivel into the wind; its smaller open end trails off downwind. Indicates both direction and force of wind.

wing loading The actual weight of the airplane and its contents that is lifted by the wing, plus any multiplication of this weight that might be imposed by additional G-loads from maneuvering.

wings The airfoil-shaped lifting surfaces of an airplane.

wing tip vortices Spiral, funnel shaped air currents that trail back and downwards from the wing tips of any plane in flight. These counter-rotating tip vortices increase in size and force according to the weight of the aircraft producing them. A light plane passing through such a wake from a large heavy plane will experience it as severe turbulence.

yaw One of the four axes about which an airplane moves in flight. The nose is said to yaw to left or right, a motion controlled by the rudder.

yoke Another common name for the **control wheel.**

INDEX